When CRICKET Was CRICKET

For dad – cricket umpire and cricket fan

First published in 2011

A catalogue record for this book is available from the British Library

ISBN: 978-0-857330-41-3

Published by Haynes Publishing, Sparkford, Yeovil,
Somerset BA22 7JJ, UK
Tel: 01963 442030 Fax: 01963 440001
Int. tel: +44 1963 442030 Int. fax: +44 1963 440001
E-mail: sales@haynes.co.uk
Website: www.haynes.co.uk

Haynes North America Inc., 861 Lawrence Drive,
Newbury Park, California 91320, USA

Images © Mirrorpix

Creative Director: Kevin Gardner
Designed for Haynes by BrainWave

Printed and bound in the US

When CRICKET Was CRICKET

A Nostalgic Look at a Century of the Greatest Game

Adam Powley

Contents

Introduction

Is there any other sport that fits nostalgia as snugly as cricket? Arguably no other pastime has such a rich tradition of wistful reminiscence as the game of bat and ball. The clichéd crack of leather upon willow, the long hot summers of a hazily remembered past, the identification of the sport with the finer aspects of a bygone age: we can all be guilty of looking at such history through rose-tinted vision, but that perception is an intrinsic part of the sport.

This book is about the game when cricket *was* cricket. You won't find many photos here of players in multi-coloured kit, or fireworks and cheerleaders, or the crash, bang, wallop of the T20 format. That all has its fine and worthwhile place in the modern sport, but this tour through decades past is about a different game. It's a celebration of a less frantic and probably more entertaining time when great cricket was created by great players rather than contrived by marketing gurus and showbiz choreographers.

This is not to say that the modern version is inferior; England's thrilling Ashes victory in 2010-11 reminded fans how exciting and captivating the game can still be. Nor does this book seek to pretend that all was sweetness and light in the past. Far from it – cricket has an occasionally tawdry and murky history as well as a gleaming and honest one. But the story here harks back to a different age, the passing of which many cricket lovers still lament. It's about players and characters, the memorable games and classic Test series, the glittering pinnacle of the sport and its humble grass roots, as it was in years gone by.

Neither is this simply a book about that conventional history, nor the minutiae of how the game has been played with exhaustively detailed statistics (though there is also plenty of all of that, with the intention to inform and entertain).

When Cricket Was Cricket is about the wider game – a celebration of the sport's customs, oddities and curiosities, and as much a fond reflection on its homespun charm as it is a familiar roll-call of glamorous personalities and events of international renown.

A note on the choice of "legends" that appear throughout the book. All such selections are inevitably subjective, based on personal preference as much as consensus regarding merit. Since cricket is a sport so open to opinion, the selection here may well please and dismay in equal measure. For the purposes of this volume, the players featured are not necessarily among the greatest, but have been included for their embodiment of an era or simply their unique appeal that ranges beyond what they achieved on the pitch. There is also the consideration of time and space – the book draws to a close in the 1990s, so some outstanding cricketers of more recent vintage, particularly from the brilliant Australian side that dominated the Test scene for a decade or more, regretfully had to be excluded. (A note also on the "Scoreboard" stats: averages have been included to give an indication of all-round career performance; some batsmen will thus for example have very high bowling averages.)

The result is that this is an affectionate tribute to, and a snapshot of, certain times and places in cricket's compelling history. Drawing on the wonderful photographs in the vast Mirrorpix archive, the book seeks to provide a glimpse of the game – and remind us all of a time when cricket really was cricket.

Adam Powley

Origins and Early Days
16th CENTURY-1919

From a match at Hampton Wick, the quintessential English cricket scene.

Cricket enjoys a lineage and heritage richer than perhaps any other team sport. Rudimentary games involving forms of bats and balls date back to **before the Norman Conquest**, and across Europe, but in terms of becoming a codified, organized pursuit, cricket has few peers. A recognizable form of the game emerged in England in the **mid- to late 16th century** – a legal case referred to a game of "krickett" played in Surrey in **1597** – before a period of retrenchment after the **English Civil War**, when strict Puritan observance of church attendance on the Sabbath meant cricketers found little time during the day of rest to indulge their hobby.

   After the Restoration, gambling amongst the nobility played an increasingly important role in English sporting life, and cricket began to receive more widespread attention – one Sussex game in **1697** attracted wagers of 50 guineas per side. Matches between notionally representative county sides were established by **1709**, while a full set of laws was drawn up in **1744** by the "London Club". A group of wealthy and powerful landowners formed the Star and Garter Club in **1784**, which evolved into the Marylebone Cricket Club (MCC), based at Lord's in **1787**. MCC rules were drawn up a year later. Class distinctions within cricket were writ large with the first "Gentleman v. Players" game at Lord's in **1806**, but with the sport spreading around

the globe as the British Empire expanded, the game began to grow out of its parochial English origins. While Sussex County Cricket Club was formally founded in **1839**, the first international cricket match took place in **1844** between Canada and America. W G Grace, the first true cricket superstar, made his debut in **1865**, and an England side toured Australia and played a nascent form of "Test" match in **1877**.

   The laws and organization of the game continued to be modified and developed – the six-ball over was formalized in **1900** (though other versions persisted), the Imperial Cricket Conference (ICC) was formed in **1909** (it was renamed the International Cricket Conference in 1965 and International Cricket Council in 1989), while the list of cricket-playing nations grew to encompass various countries throughout the empire and beyond. By the time of the **First World War**, cricket had evolved from its age-old rural roots in the shires of southern England to become a global phenomenon, played, watched and enjoyed by millions.

When CRICKET Was CRICKET

7

Hambledon Cricket Club is often cited as the "cradle of cricket". It was not the first club side, and actually came to prominence due to wealthy and powerful patrons in London, but its rural village surroundings in Hampshire has made it the focal point for many histories tracing the evolution of the game.

The Bat & Ball Inn in Hyden Farm Lane is pictured circa 1910, next to the famous ground at the wonderfully evocative Broadhalfpenny Down.

BELOW: Archdeacon Fearon of Winchester, speaking from the monument to cricketers at Hambledon in September 1908.

Scenes from yesteryear: women were keen players of the game and, according to one (often discredited) legend, pioneered the introduction of overarm bowling due to their hooped skirts. In the 1906 match between Cambridge and Royston, a Miss Holden demonstrated the arts of batting (below); the 1904 Lancashire line-up (right) featured (left to right) Heaps, Cuttell, Sladen, Tyldesley, Hallows, Kermode and Sharpe; in an illustration of the 1880 Test against Australia at the Oval (opposite), Lord Harris saved a four; again at the Oval, a match between 11 one-armed and 11 one-legged pensioners of Greenwich Hospital was played in 1862; the scoreboard proudly displays Yorkshire's record score against Warwickshire set in May 1896 (below opposite).

Match
Lord Harris (Capt. of English Team) saving a 4"

LEFT: Revivals of old forms of cricket and playing attire are a common occurrence in the modern game. In 2010, the 150th anniversary of village sides Whickham and Percy Main was marked by playing a match to 1860 laws and by donning 1860 garb, including caps, waistcoats and cravats.

> *In strength they were about equal to third-class English teams and the result of their visit was satisfactory and encouraging to them in every respect.*
>
> W G Grace

ABOVE: The first foreign side to tour England came, not surprisingly, from Australia, where the game had established its deepest roots away from the mother country. But this wasn't a team made up of colonial players whose origins lay in Europe. Instead, it was a group of Aborigines who in 1868 pioneered a trail that generations of patriotic Australians have since followed.

The touring side was drawn from a number of so-called "blackfellas" who had taken up the game after seeing white farm workers on sheep stations in Western Victoria play cricket. The touring party played at over 40 grounds around England, including Lord's, attracting huge crowds that were thrillingly entertained by the visitors' style of play.

Collector's edition: relics from cricket's past, particularly the so-called "golden age" of the 1900s, are hugely popular and command considerable prices at auction. The 1903 Test match ball (above left) was valued at £1,500 in 1998, and *The Empire's Cricketers Book* from 1905 (above right) valued at up to £21,500.

ABOVE: Match-fixing in cricket is nothing new (one leading player, William Lambert, was banned for supposedly committing the offence in 1817 by not trying hard enough), and with gambling such an integral part of the sport's early years, the notion that the game has always represented all that is good about English society and culture is somewhat exaggerated. Nonetheless, early in the sport's history, the qualities of decency, honesty and probity stuck, and came to embody the "best of British". In 1920, revelations that a man accused of murder had captained a cricket team implied a sharp contrast in character. Harold Greenwood (second left, seated) skippered Kidwelly Town Cricket Club in 1909, and it was this role that was presented alongside his supposed dastardliness during his sensational trial, in which he was accused and later acquitted of killing his first wife.

Top ho! A 1908 match at Richmond gets the top-hat treatment.

The Estimable W G

Cricket's first true superstar was a burly and bearded native of Bristol, who rose from provincial county competition to become one of the great sporting heroes of his generation and known around the world. Few figures come to define their sport, but in the later half of the 19th century and into the 20th, William Gilbert Grace was the biggest performer and personality in cricket bar none.

The highlights of his extraordinary career are many and varied. He scored his first century for England (against Surrey) aged just 18. During the match this accomplished athlete was given permission to nip off and win a three-quarter mile race at Crystal Palace. Between 1868 and 1880, he led the first-class batting averages no fewer than 10 times. In 1873 he became the first player to score more than 1,000 runs (in total 2,139) and take 100 wickets (106). Though he is more readily identified as a batsman, he was a genuine all-rounder, and was the first bowler to take 2,000 wickets.

Grace's statistical record at Test level was impressive but not exceptional – though it has to be borne in mind the circumstances of how cricket was played at the time. Well-prepared wickets were a rarity; the good Doctor did not make his Test debut until he was 32; four-ball overs (up to 1889) enabled bowlers to be more potent (and little in way of protection was provided against their deliveries).

It should also be noted that Grace was no paragon of unblemished virtue. He was often confrontational and curmudgeonly (notably with umpires), had a reputation for cunning, and his ruthless professionalism belied his "Gentleman" status. Indeed, his lucrative "expenses" rendered his claims to be an amateur largely meaningless. However, his reputation transcends that of mere statistics and his apparent flaws. Grace's 43-year career was one of unprecedented success and renown, and he captivated the sporting public like no other. Adding W G's name to the team sheet was a guarantee to add thousands to the gate (along with thruppence to the admission price), and it is telling that nearly a century after his death, his is still one of the first names to appear in any list of cricketing greats.

He orchestrated the folk music of cricket.

Neville Cardus

–LEGENDS–

W G Grace

RIGHT: The great and the good, like the Prince of Wales (the Duke of Windsor), all wanted to associate themselves with the great superstar.

BELOW: The unmistakable figure of W G Grace in the England line-up before the Test match against Australia at Trent Bridge, 1st June 1899. Back row, left to right: Umpire Titchmarsh, G H Hirst, T Hayward, W Gunn, J T Hearne, W Storer, W Brockwell. Middle row: C B Fry, Prince Ranjitsinhji, Grace (capt.), F S Jackson, Umpire Barlow. Seated, front: W Rhodes, J T Tyldesley.

CRICKET
–SCORECARD–

W G Grace

Name: William Gilbert Grace

Born: 1848

Died: 1915

Test appearances: 22

Batting average: 32.29

Bowling average: 26.22

First-class batting average: 39.45

First-class bowling average: 18.14

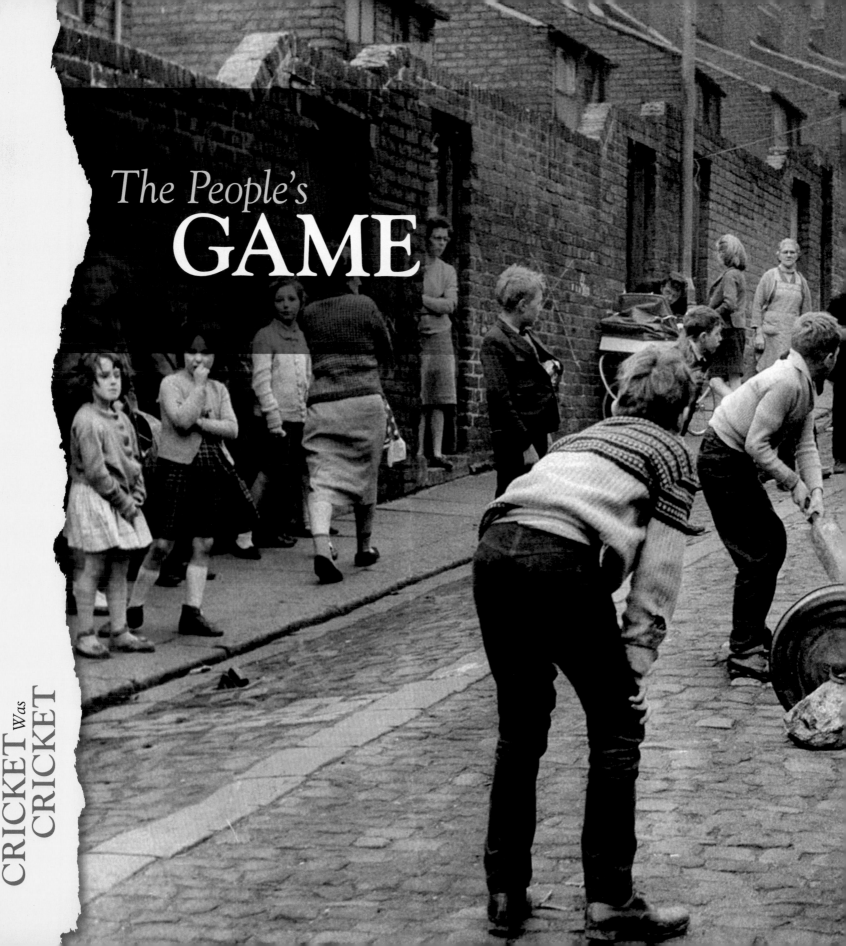

The People's GAME

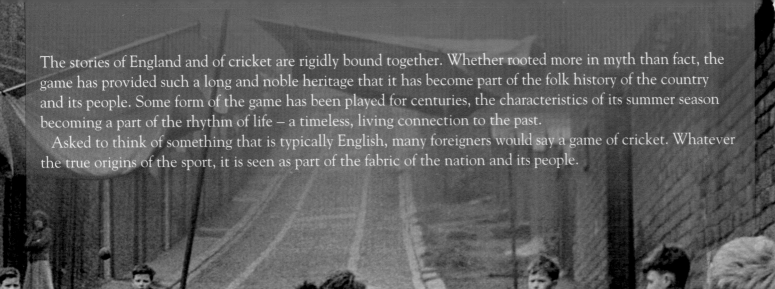

The stories of England and of cricket are rigidly bound together. Whether rooted more in myth than fact, the game has provided such a long and noble heritage that it has become part of the folk history of the country and its people. Some form of the game has been played for centuries, the characteristics of its summer season becoming a part of the rhythm of life – a timeless, living connection to the past.

Asked to think of something that is typically English, many foreigners would say a game of cricket. Whatever the true origins of the sport, it is seen as part of the fabric of the nation and its people.

The Scotswood area of Newcastle in 1970: even in the most challenging of urban environments, kids have found a place to play cricket.

Part of cricket's appeal has been its popularity across social divides. Yet the sport has also laid those distinctions bare. The young urchins playing a game in London's East End of the 1950s (left) had to make do with pads made out of paper, while the well-heeled boys of St Chad's Cathedral School enjoyed altogether more salubrious surroundings while playing in the shadow of Lichfield Cathedral in 1959.

It Takes a Village...

The origins of the game lie in the village sides whose names may have been first recorded in the 18th century but whose origins probably date back far further. The keenly contested but sportingly observed match on the village green may be one of cricket's most enduring clichés, but it rings true: the game was established at a time when the population was overwhelmingly rural-based, and, without such pastoral roots, it is questionable whether the sport would have been interpreted as such an integral part of England's identity.

RIGHT INSET: Scoring for fun with Meopham's homely facilities.

> *In every English village a cricket field is as much a part of the landscape as the old church.*
>
> Neville Cardus

The village of Meopham in Kent plays host to one of the oldest village sides, first formally recognized in 1776 – the year the United States of America was born – making the Meopham team as old as a nation.

Cricket has appealed to young and old: with an average age of 77 not out, a group of Chelsea Pensioners (above) took in the England versus New Zealand match at Lord's in 1973; family life in Oldham 1952 (left) saw a young lad oiling his bat and perhaps dreaming of being Jack Hobbs or Len Hutton.

The political Test... Cricket has often reflected wider political and social affairs. Ted Dexter batted gamely for the Conservative Party in 1964 by contesting a parliamentary seat in Cardiff, losing out to future Prime Minister Jim Callaghan (and injuring his foot a year later, left). On the beer-and-sandwiches side of cricket's political divide, TUC leader Vic Feather (above) padded up at a conference match in Blackpool in 1970.

At school, in the workplace, in the street: people have played cricket wherever they can, even overcoming physical handicaps to do so.

BELOW: A group of young lads play cricket up against a backstreet wall in 1939. Note the boy with the artificial leg.

ABOVE: Children on crutches play cricket at Hampstead.

LEFT: Leg before bottle? Geoffrey Williams, captain and opening bat for Ynysgerwn Cricket Club, took time out to get some practice in during a break at work in a depot in Aberdulais, Neath, in 1979.

The 1920s

After the slaughter of the First World War, in which over 30 county cricketers lost their lives, many people sought a degree of solace in the familiar comforts of cricket. The resumption of the summer game seemed to symbolize a return to something approaching normality – the old order restored. Yet time was not standing still. This was the decade in which the game's global reach extended: a flurry of nations joined the ICC, while a number of grounds in exotic locations made their debuts on the Test circuit.

Back home in the land that gave birth to the sport, Glamorgan joined the county fold in **1921**, while Jack Hobbs made his 100th century, helping Surrey to victory over Somerset in **1923**. **Two years later**, Yorkshire won the county championship for the fourth year in succession. But just to show that it was not all business as usual, a sure sign of progress came with the establishment of the English Women's Cricket Association in **1926**.

Meanwhile, **1924** witnessed the first ever first-class match in Sri Lanka, or Ceylon as it was then known. The West Indies announced their membership of the international fold with their first Test visit to Lord's in **1928**, the same year Don Bradman made his Test debut for Australia (and Walter Hammond took 10 catches in one match playing for Gloucestershire against Surrey, while scoring a century in each innings). For a series of games between **1929 and 1930**, the Queen's Park Oval, Port of Spain, the Basin Reserve, Wellington, and the Kensington Oval, Bridgetown, all hosted their first ever Test matches. **1929** also saw the formation of the Board of Control for Cricket in India, two

Charles Burgess (more commonly known as C B) Fry was one of the foremost personalities of cricket's "golden age", and was still playing at first-class level in the early 1920s. A prodigious all-round sportsman, he excelled not only at cricket with England and Hampshire, but played for England and Southampton at football, and set a world long-jump record that lasted for 21 years – a boy's-own adventurer if ever there was. He was even a contender for the throne of Albania.

Although he was in his sporting dotage in 1921, he was still a big draw wherever he appeared, whether in the nets or signing autographs while puffing on a pipe – a stereotypical "toff" and a living symbol of a pre-First World War sporting era. C B was something of an anachronism, however; "The Almighty" was one of a passing breed as cricket tentatively embraced a more modern age.

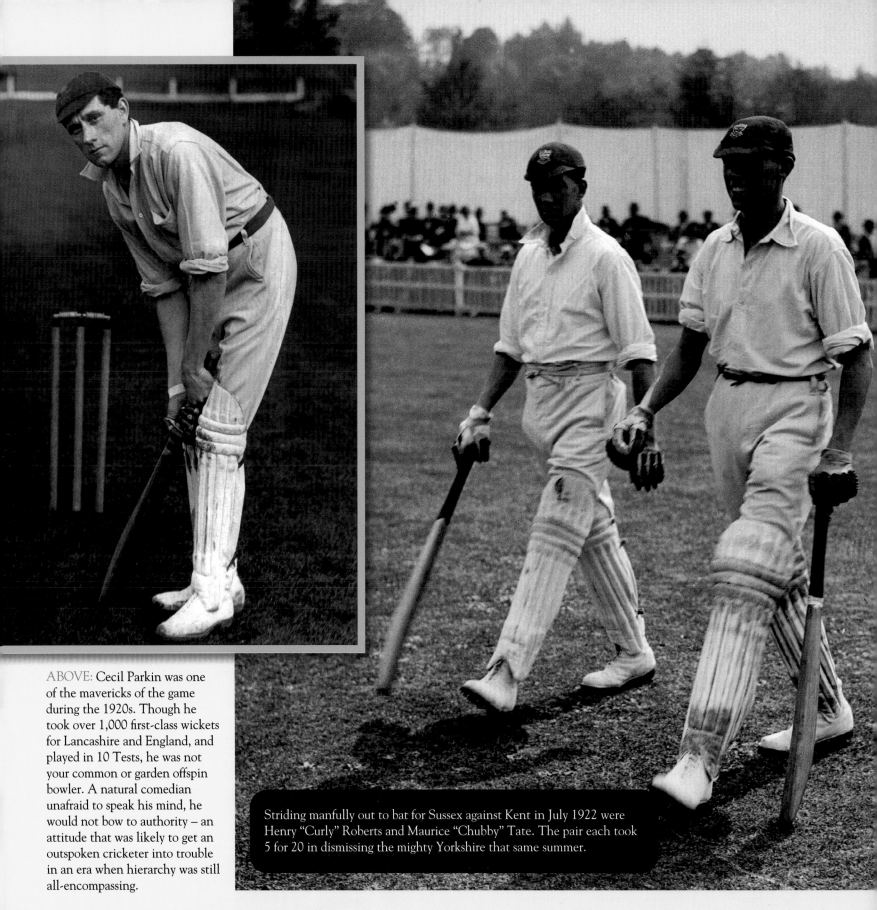

ABOVE: Cecil Parkin was one of the mavericks of the game during the 1920s. Though he took over 1,000 first-class wickets for Lancashire and England, and played in 10 Tests, he was not your common or garden offspin bowler. A natural comedian unafraid to speak his mind, he would not bow to authority – an attitude that was likely to get an outspoken cricketer into trouble in an era when hierarchy was still all-encompassing.

Striding manfully out to bat for Sussex against Kent in July 1922 were Henry "Curly" Roberts and Maurice "Chubby" Tate. The pair each took 5 for 20 in dismissing the mighty Yorkshire that same summer.

ABOVE: Living to the ripe old age of 92, Percy Fender was one of the last survivors of pre-First World War cricket, and one of Surrey's greatest players. Seen here in 1920 about to receive a hearty handshake from an admiring fan, he also featured in 13 Test matches.

LEFT: The famous Old Father Time weather vane at Lord's, donated to the MCC by the architect Sir Herbert Baker in 1926.

–LEGENDS–

Sir Jack Hobbs

Jack Hobbs remains one of the greatest ever batsmen – certainly one that holds company with the likes of Bradman, Richards and, from the modern era, Lara and Tendulkar. Whatever the conditions, whatever type of bowling he faced, Hobbs was a composed, accomplished craftsman at the wicket. He had an enormous appetite for run-getting, with a first-class career total of 61,760 runs and 199 centuries.

A true sportsman in the way he played the game, it is said that Hobbs would have scored many more centuries had he not surrendered his wicket so often once he passed three figures. Factoring in that he missed several years of his prime because of the First World War and that he often played on unprotected "sticky" wickets, his feats become all the more remarkable.

Knighted in 1953, "The Master", as he was known, was the prime example of the pre-war sporting hero. He was self-taught and rose from modest origins in Cambridge to become an inspiration to millions of boys, all of them wide-eyed in admiration for the great man's achievements, both at county level for Surrey and as the finest opener for England the nation has seen. In *Wisden*'s famous poll of the five greatest cricketers of the 20th century, he is placed at number three – the only Englishman in the selection.

> *He's going to be a good 'un.*
>
> W G Grace on the 22-year-old Hobbs

Autograph hunters flocked to secure the Jack Hobbs signature.

BELOW: Hobbs completing his 106th century in first-class cricket against Derbyshire at the Oval.

CRICKET
— SCORECARD —

Sir Jack Hobbs

Name: Sir Jack Hobbs

Born: 1882

Died: 1963

Test appearances: 61

Batting average: 56.94

Bowling average: 165.00

First-class batting average: 50.70

First-class bowling average: 25.04

Walking out with Herbert Sutcliffe to face the Aussies in June 1926. The pair formed one of the most effective of all opening partnerships. Hobbs scored the last of his 12 Ashes' centuries at the age of 46.

Taking the acclaim of an enthusiastic crowd in 1923, Surrey's barnstorming bowler Bill Hitch wended his way home after his man-of-the-match performance in the tussle with Kent at Blackheath.

Sussex cricketer John Langridge in action in the nets. One of the best English cricketers of the 20th century never to play a Test match, he turned out for Sussex from 1928 to 1955, but came into contention for the national side at the worst possible moment, earning selection for the 1939–40 tour of India that was postponed because of the war.

A Passage to England

Long before the days of jet travel made travel times between Australia and England a matter of hours, cricketers had a lengthy and often arduous journey to make in order to play in Ashes matches. For the 1926 series, Australian cricketers Clarrie Grimmett (above), Jack Ryder and Sam Everett (right) made a sight-seeing stopover in Egypt in April. The holiday-snap happiness was not repeated on the tour. Several of the Australian players succumbed to illness and injury, rain ruined much of the fixtures programme and the Aussies lost the Test series 1-0.

The Social
SCENE

Old Harrovians huzzah and hurrah at the 1914
Eton v. Harrow match at Lord's – a poignant scene
given the horrors of warfare soon to come.

With its aristocratic antecedents that lay at the heart of much of the early game, a considerable element of cricket has always been reserved as something of a rich man's plaything. Polite society loved to socialize at the great cricket events of the summer calendar – opening day in the first Test at Lord's, the Varsity match between Oxford and Cambridge and, of course, that parade for the upper classes, the Eton versus Harrow fixture.

"Eton and Harrow" was first played at Lord's (on the old Dorset Square site) in 1805, 18 years after the enterprising Thomas Lord had entered into an agreement with the aristocrats and nobility of the MCC to create an enclosed ground. From 1822 the match became an annual fixture, and by 1912 (below) was a firmly established date in the social diary for the well-heeled and well-connected.

Even into the late 20th century, the sartorial idiosyncrasies of the Eton v. Harrow game were alive and well, as seen here in 1966.

ABOVE: Being seen at a cricket match has long been a good piece of political PR. Mrs Baldwin, wife of Prime Minister Stanley Baldwin, turned up with parasol in hand for the 1923 Eton v. Harrow game.

RIGHT: The Varsity match between Oxford and Cambridge has also been a must-see event for the well-to-do, as with this scene from 1914.

A E R Gilligan, a fine captain of England and Sussex and later president of the MCC, and A W Carr (see pages 52–3), another former England skipper, take the acclaim of a respectful crowd at Scarborough for a Gentleman versus Players match in September 1925.

This curious fixture was a mirror to the strange but deep-seated stratification – not to say snobbery – of the English game. Amateur "Gentlemen" were primarily drawn from the ranks of the rich and powerful, and portrayed as defenders of all that was pure and noble about the sport. The "Players" were the professionals who tended to be recruited from the lower orders. The matches between the two groups gave such distinctions, and the naked class prejudice that underpinned them, official status: the two teams would enter a ground via separate entrances, changed in different dressing rooms, and even had to sit at separate tables with different menus at lunch.

Despite huge changes in the sport and beyond, the fixture persisted right up to 1962, when the last game was played, coincidentally at Scarborough.

> [the professional is] fagged and jaded…
> spoiled by feasting and flattery
>
> Reverend James Pycroft, 1851

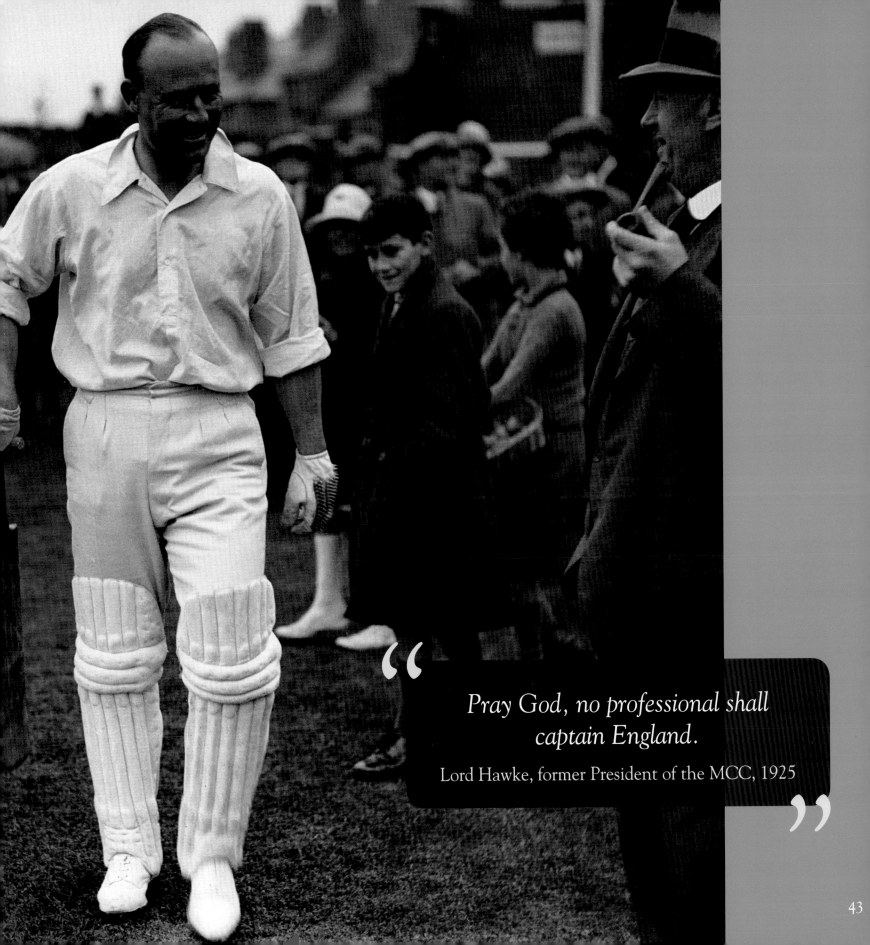

> *Pray God, no professional shall captain England.*
>
> Lord Hawke, former President of the MCC, 1925

As befits the vaunted position cricket holds in the national identity, the monarchy has often been seen to be seen in association with the sport.

Sir Don Bradman (centre) discussed the finer points of batting with King George VI and Queen Elizabeth (later the Queen Mother) at Balmoral in 1948.

RIGHT: Sending down a challenging delivery was Prince Philip, Duke of Edinburgh, playing at Arundel Castle in August 1953.

King George V greeted the West Indies' Learie Constantine at Nottingham, in July 1928.

LEFT: "And what do you do?" Queen Elizabeth II consoled Australia's Rick McCosker who had broken his jaw in the opening day of the Australia v. England Test in 1977, a match played during the monarch's Silver Jubilee celebrations down under.

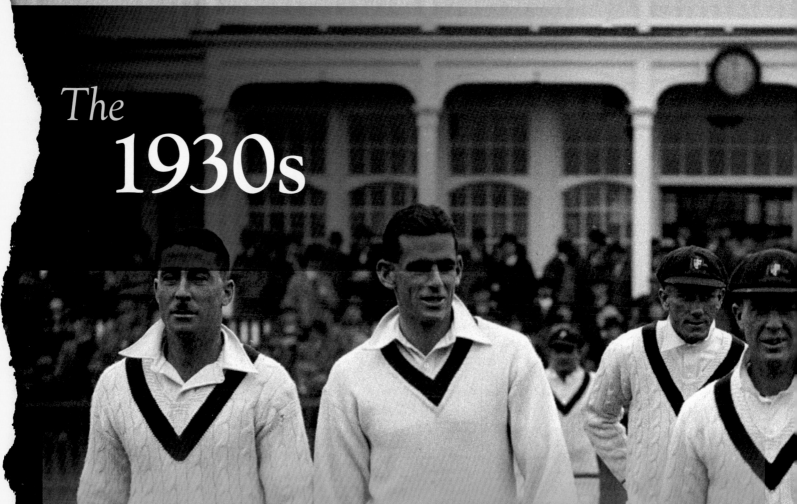

The
1930s

The 1930s was a period of great upheaval in the wider world and cricket also experienced its fair share of change, including the emergence of more sides from the colonies, such as India and the West Indies, the advent of women's Test matches, and the very first televised cricket. But while many of the familiar stars shone, the dominant figure was a former country lad who would become by common consent the greatest cricketer of all time.

The decade began with the admirable achievements of a cricketer nearing the autumn of his career, as England's Andrew Sandham notched the first ever Test triple century against the West Indies in Kingston in **1930**. Was the change in stump height from 28 inches to 27 and width to nine inches in **1931** a response to such mammoth knocks?

In the **1931-32** series against South Africa in Australia, the Woolloongabba ground in Brisbane – later to be more commonly known as the Gabba – staged its first Test. Later in **1932**, India made their Test debut at Lord's. Famous players such as K S Ranjitsinhji and the Nawab of Pataudi had in eras past had to don English whites in order to play at the highest level. In **1934-35** the Ranji trophy, named in honour of Ranjitsinhji, was inaugurated as India's pre-eminent national competition.

Earlier in **1932** began one of the most notorious Test series in cricket history (see page 88), but an altogether less controversial and more sedate affair was played in **1937-38** with the last first-class match to date in South America: Argentina against Sir Thomas Brinkman's XI. As one aspect of cricket faded, another continued its development: **1937** saw the first women's cricket Test match in England, against Australia at Northampton.

Within the men's county game in England, Kent's Arthur Fagg earned his place in history with an unbeaten double century in each innings of a **1938** game against Essex – the only time the feat has been achieved at first-class level. Sadly, television cameras were not on hand to record Fagg's exploits, but they were in use in the same year for the second Test of the Ashes series at Lord's between England and Australia, broadcast live on the fledgling BBC Service. The few viewers were later able to see Len Hutton's world-record setting 364 from the Oval. It was a modernizing sign of things to come, but in **1939** there was an example of the old ways, with a 10-day match between South Africa and England at Durban, eventually abandoned as a draw – the longest Test ever played.

The Aussies are coming... Australian dominance in world cricket was nothing new – the victory over England in 1882 had confirmed that the balance of power would not always reside as if by God-given right in the mother country – but the tourists taking to the field against Leicestershire in August 1930 were a new force to be reckoned with. Among them were, left to right: Fairfax, Ponsford, Jackson, Kippax, Harwood, Wall and V Richardson.

Looking dapper in their blazers and baggy greens, the Australian touring party of 1930 lined up for their photo call.

BATSMAN
1
224

TOTAL
555
CAUGHT

BATSMAN
2
313

WICKETS
LAST PLAYER
11 BOWLERS 7

Taking to the field against Essex, Australia's Bill Woodfull (above, left) and Bill Ponsford came out to open the batting on 7th May 1930 at the County Ground, Leyton. Matches, including internationals, were played at this much loved venue from 1885 right up until 1977. It was the site of the then world-record opening stand of 555 secured by Herbert Sutcliffe and Percy Holmes of Yorkshire in 1932, displayed on the homely scoreboard (left). The record stood for 44 years and is still the highest-scoring partnership in domestic English cricket.

The Greatest

The finest batsman of all time? Unquestionably. The best cricketer ever? There are few, if any, rivals. One of the truly great sportsmen, whatever the discipline? Certainly. Don Bradman, like W G Grace before him, defined his era, but his achievements and influence exceed even that of his illustrious predecessor and eclipse those of his successors. It is unlikely there will ever be another quite like the Don.

Voted as the best in *Wisden's* poll of the greatest 20th-century players, and the embodiment of the nuggety, never-say-die Aussie who plays to win by fair means, Bradman appeared in only a relatively small number of Tests (52) but his prolific, relentless scoring elevated him to immortal status. For a period during the early 1930s he was almost unplayable – the Bodyline tactic was largely devised to negate his threat (see pages 88–9) and even then was only partially successful. It is said that for such a fluent, magnificent yet almost unorthodox batsman he was naturally gifted, but that diminishes the hard work of repetition, effort and application he devoted himself to from an early age, as he grew up in New South Wales. Other batsmen may have possessed similar talents, but none could match Bradman for putting such skills into practice and with such faultless concentration.

A private man off the pitch, he earned the goodwill of all who had the privilege to see him play. On the occasion of his final Test match in 1948, he walked to the crease to a standing ovation at the Oval, set to secure the astonishing average of 100 or more. He was bowled for a duck, second ball, by Eric Hollies, leaving Bradman marooned on 99.94. But what a record to depart on! Bradman was anything but average.

> "He was never overpowering with his deeds, he was meek in some ways and did not thrust it down people's throats. Today's players could learn a lot from him.
>
> Brian Close"

–LEGENDS–

Sir Don Bradman

ABOVE: The 21-year-old Bradman doing what he did best in 1929 – scoring runs.

BELOW: Bradman autographs one of his bats, which was auctioned in aid of the Lord Mayor of London's Children Fund in 1948. The Don was made a knight a year later. "I would have preferred to remain mister," he said.

CRICKET
–SCORECARD–

Sir Don Bradman

Name: Sir Don Bradman

Born: 1908

Died: 2001

Test appearances: 52

Batting average: 99.94

Bowling average: 36.00

First-class batting average: 95.14

First-class bowling average: 37.97

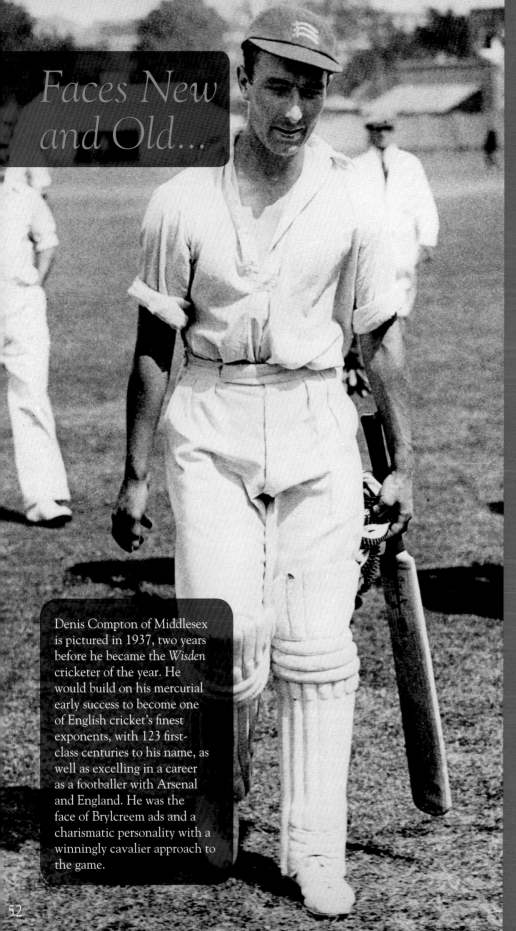

Denis Compton of Middlesex
is pictured in 1937, two years
before he became the *Wisden*
cricketer of the year. He
would build on his mercurial
early success to become one
of English cricket's finest
exponents, with 123 first-
class centuries to his name, as
well as excelling in a career
as a footballer with Arsenal
and England. He was the
face of Brylcreem ads and a
charismatic personality with a
winningly cavalier approach to
the game.

ABOVE: Cricket could be a very serious business, and
the rigours of leadership were written all over the face of
Nottinghamshire skipper Arthur Carr in 1933. Controversy
dogged the latter stages of Carr's career – he was seen as one
of the architects of the Bodyline strategy (see page 88) and his
steadfast defence of his Notts bowlers Harold Larwood and Bill
Voce led to Carr's eventual removal as the county's captain.

ABOVE: Cricketers and their sweethearts were not quite the Posh and Becks of their day but still made the news. Bowling a maiden over was Kent and England's Leslie Ames, enjoying his nuptials with Leonie Muriel File at Elham under a cricket-bat guard of honour in May 1930.

The Windies of Change

The 1930s was the decade in which the West Indies began to make their mark on international cricket. Representative sides had been formed as early as the 1880s, but having made their Test debut in 1928, the succeeding years saw players from the islands make more of an impact. Trinidad's brilliant all-rounder Learie Constantine pioneered a trail that many others would follow.

RIGHT: All-rounder Ben Sealey in 1933.

LEFT: Jackie Grant, captain of the West Indian touring side in 1933. White men led the side until the 1950s, and the likes of Frank Worrell took charge. Grant went on to become a missionary once he retired from the sport.

BELOW: Ivan Barrow (left) the first West Indian to score a century in England (at Old Trafford in 1933) and Oscar Da Costa, a charismatic player who carried a rubber stamp engraved with his signature so he could jokingly save time signing autographs. He died in 1936, aged just 29.

Enthusiastic crowds gathered to see the West Indies in action, as illustrated in this bucolic scene from the match against Norfolk at Norwich in August 1933.

RIGHT: The Sabina Park scoreboard in Kingston, Jamaica, proudly displays England's (and Sandham's) mammoth run haul from the first innings of the fourth Test in April 1930. The match was drawn.

War and
PEACE

As a second conflict within a generation raged across the world, regular cricket was once again largely put on hold. Lord's was damaged by bombing, and with players signed up for active service (many cricketers lost their lives during the Second World War, including 10 Test players), the analogies of staunchly defending a wicket or sending down a knockout delivery had a strangely apposite resonance.

Hedley Verity, a magnificent bowler for Yorkshire and England, took seven Sussex wickets for just nine runs in the final moments of peacetime county cricket on 1st September 1939. As a captain in the Green Howards, Verity saw action from North Africa to Italy but was mortally wounded in a corn field in Catania, four years to the day after his final brilliant performance on the cricket field. Close to death in an enemy hospital he said, "I may have played my last innings for Yorkshire." His last words to his men were "Keep going!"

Even in a London ravaged by Hitler's bombs, play continued. John Hudd (with the bat) was a seven-year-old boy from Canning Town in the East End whose home in Clarkson Street had been destroyed in the Blitz in 1941. But with his little brothers, Billy aged six (behind the wicket) and Freddie, aged four, at leg slip, John still managed to metaphorically knock the Nazis for six (before being clean bowled to the delight of his younger siblings).

ABOVE: Cricketers being cricketers, devotees of the game would find a way to get in a few overs whatever the circumstances, as with these gas mask-wearing sportsmen in 1941.

RIGHT: Action from the crunch meeting between the Auxiliary Fire Service and their female WAFS counterparts at Clapham in September 1941.

Miller in action in the nets.

–LEGENDS–

Keith Miller

A magnificent all-rounder in life as well as on the cricket pitch, Australia's Keith Miller was one of the most charismatic of all the great players. A dashing idol with film star looks and an ebullient, witty, gregarious personality who lived life to the full, he entertained and enraptured post-war crowds who took him to their hearts. How appropriate it was that Miller was born in a town called Sunshine.

Miller was an outstanding fast bowler and a batsman of no less influential quality. His bowling partnership with Ray Lindwall was one of the most devastating in world cricket, his glorious and mighty stroke play a joy to behold. But it was not just his considerable playing talents that made him so popular. The crowds took to Miller in no small part because of his courageous war record. As an RAAF fighter pilot during the war, he had experienced danger first-hand, and the perspective that gave to his general approach to life struck a chord with his many admirers.

Flying Mosquitoes with 169 Squadron he once narrowly escaped death. "Nearly stumps drawn, that time," he wryly commented.

Miller usually took to the field with a smile on his face and played with relaxed panache. His reputation as the life and soul of the party only added to his allure. A very keen betting man, it was said he once flew down the home straights of Ascot and Goodwood in order to closely assess the going.

> " *Pressure is a Messerschmitt up your arse; playing cricket is not.* "
>
> Keith Miller

CRICKET
–SCORECARD–

Keith Miller

Name: Keith Miller

Born: 1919

Died: 2004

Test appearances: 55

Batting average: 36.97

Bowling average: 22.97

First-class batting average: 48.90

First-class bowling average: 22.30

LEFT: Wally Hammond was England's outstanding batsman of the 1930s, but he enjoyed a mixed career swansong once cricket resumed after the war. He led the England Test side to defeat in 1946–7, yet at the age of 43, headed the overall first-class averages in 1946 with 84.90.

BELOW: In 1947, members of the England Test team signed autographs in Adelaide. Left to right: Ames, unknown, Larwood, Mr C Toone (the team's manager), Hammond (standing with cigar), Sutcliffe, Tyldesley, Freeman and Geary.

With the end of hostilities still so fresh in the mind, Britons sought the comforting joys of cricket, whether on Blackpool beach in August 1946 (above), on a village track near Littlehampton in 1946 with many hands making light work of a spot of rolling (right), or during a scorching hot day in Shadwell in July 1948 (opposite right) with a young lad taking a drinks break.

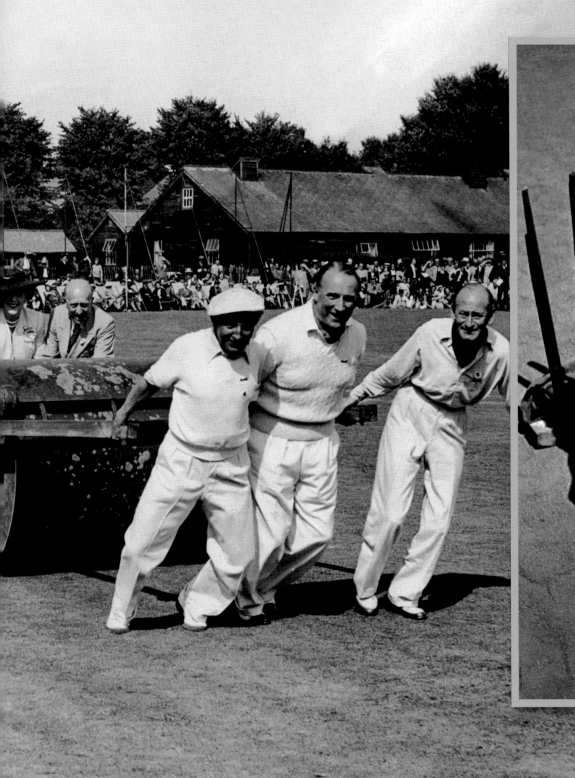

Peace in our time...
A huge crowd basks
in the glorious
sunshine of an English
cricketing summer.
A scene to warm the
hearts of a nation
battered by war,
from the Third Test
between England and
New Zealand at Old
Trafford in July 1949.

The 1948 Glamorgan side that brought the county championship to Wales for the first time.

The 1950s

Cricket's second golden age? The nostalgia for the 1950s might suggest that this was the era in which the game was arguably at its most enjoyable. Relatively strong and evenly matched sides at Test level, teams stuffed with great players whose shining reputations persist to this day, bumper crowds and the optimism of the era in which, it was claimed, we had "never had it so good". It was certainly a good era for Test bowlers such as Trueman, Laker, Lindwall, Miller, Ramadhin, Valentine and Gibbs: this was the best decade for the pacemen, mediums and spinners, with a collective average figure of just 28.54 for all Test wickets taken in the decade (according to statistics compiled by cricinfo.com).

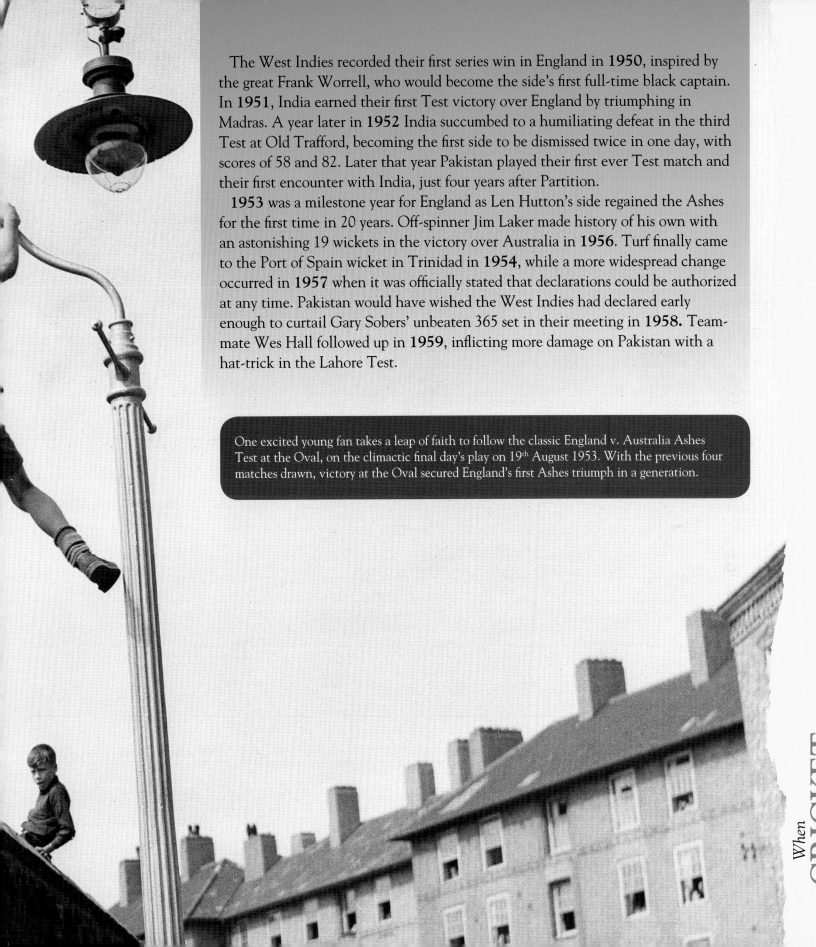

The West Indies recorded their first series win in England in **1950**, inspired by the great Frank Worrell, who would become the side's first full-time black captain. In **1951**, India earned their first Test victory over England by triumphing in Madras. A year later in **1952** India succumbed to a humiliating defeat in the third Test at Old Trafford, becoming the first side to be dismissed twice in one day, with scores of 58 and 82. Later that year Pakistan played their first ever Test match and their first encounter with India, just four years after Partition.

1953 was a milestone year for England as Len Hutton's side regained the Ashes for the first time in 20 years. Off-spinner Jim Laker made history of his own with an astonishing 19 wickets in the victory over Australia in **1956**. Turf finally came to the Port of Spain wicket in Trinidad in **1954**, while a more widespread change occurred in **1957** when it was officially stated that declarations could be authorized at any time. Pakistan would have wished the West Indies had declared early enough to curtail Gary Sobers' unbeaten 365 set in their meeting in **1958.** Teammate Wes Hall followed up in **1959**, inflicting more damage on Pakistan with a hat-trick in the Lahore Test.

One excited young fan takes a leap of faith to follow the classic England v. Australia Ashes Test at the Oval, on the climactic final day's play on 19th August 1953. With the previous four matches drawn, victory at the Oval secured England's first Ashes triumph in a generation.

The Madding Crowd

Crowds flocked to the great cricketing venues around the world and no more so than in England, where the nip and tuck of the 1953 Ashes series captured the imagination of the nation.

Such was the enthusiasm of spectators to ensure that they were there to witness first-hand the thrilling conclusion to the series in the fifth, final and deciding Test at the Oval that many queued overnight. In the event they needn't have worried. The popular belief that the gates would be shut and leave thousands locked out did not materialize in reality as many fans stayed away thinking they had no chance of admission. In the end the crowd was 26,300, well within the Oval's capacity.

Long stop and short leg... Outside Headingley, two enterprising spectators strived to get a view of the fourth Test proceedings.

ABOVE: Excited schoolboys kept themselves amused as they eagerly awaited the gates to open at Headingley.

Rain didn't stop play: trying out a new drying machine at Edgbaston in 1955. Advances in pitch treatments were continuing apace, but uncovered "sticky" wickets (tracks exposed to rain and then hot sun which could be lethal for batsmen) were still around well into the 1970s.

ABOVE: Groundsman Harry Williams whose all-out efforts saved the third Test match between England and Pakistan at Manchester in July 1954 from being a complete wash-out. Williams had been a groundsman for 20 years at Old Trafford.

ABOVE: East Moseley Cricket Club's proximity to the River Thames had its occupational hazards for a dog called Pat, whose job it was to retrieve cricket balls from the water. In just one season in 1951, Pat recovered 448 balls. An impressive innings all of his own.

RIGHT: Inside the Long Room – not the famous chamber at cricket HQ at Lord's but the Long Room of Lancashire CCC in 1958. As an indicator that clubs were looking to exploit commercial opportunities, the venue was available for hire along with new rooms in extensions to the club pavilion at Old Trafford.

ABOVE: Harry Makepeace rang in the new season at Old Trafford in April 1951, pealing Lancashire CCC's freshly restored bell.

Practice Makes Perfect

We've all heard of the concept of putting pressure on in the field, but this scene from April 1959 suggested something altogether more drastic. Rest assured, Somerset CCC were not taking desperate measures – the army-style drill routine with rifles was coach George Lambert's idea to loosen up arms and wrists for the upcoming season.

LEFT: Women reputedly pioneered the development of overarm bowling and the girls taking a cricketing evening class at Tower Bridge Institute in May 1953 continued a fine tradition.

BELOW: Stan Worthington, the old Derbyshire and England player coaching for Lancashire in 1952, and then recently appointed assistant coach to the MCC, demonstrated a new grip to fast bowler Brian Statham.

Yorkshire coaches Maurice Leyland (left) and Arthur Mitchell explained the workings of a traditional slip-catching cradle to colts during a 1951 training session.

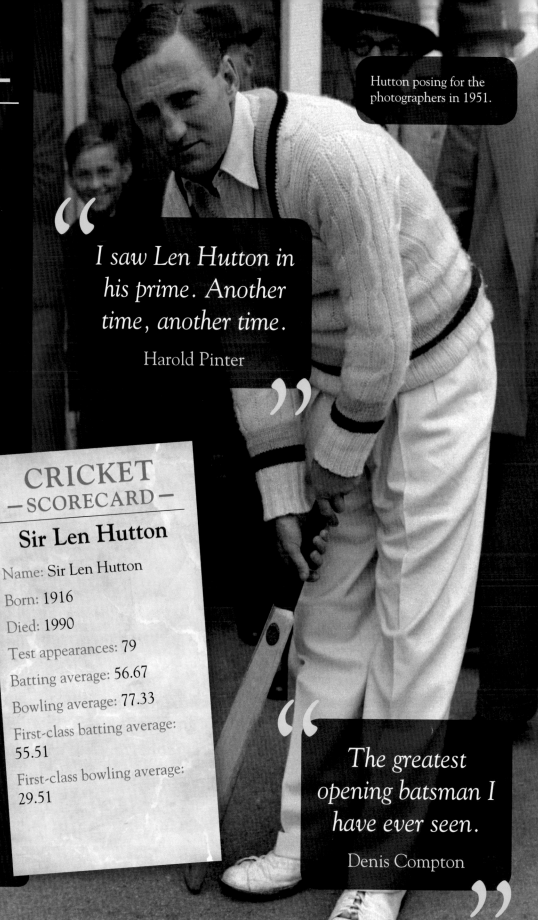

–LEGENDS–

Sir Len Hutton

For a player so clearly identified with the halcyon days of more "traditional" cricket, Len Hutton was actually something of a trailblazer. When he led England in the 1952 Test against India on his home county ground of Headingley, Hutton became his country's first professional captain. He is also regarded by many as the best captain England have ever had, and few would dispute his claim to be one of the finest opening batsmen in all cricket's long and eventful history.

Hutton was a classical batsman, beautifully measured in his stroke — play and boasting superb technique. Watching Hutton in action in his prime was, for many impressionable schoolboys of the era, one of their most cherished memories. And when some of those boys grew up to become writers and journalists, it's small wonder that Hutton often became the central subject of their tributes to the sport, with his world record of 364 against Australia in 1938 a particular highlight.

His appeal lay not only in his qualities as a cricketer but his character as well. He was brave (he fought back from a wartime accidental injury that left his left arm two inches shorter than his right), revitalized an England side with his inspirational example, and was a true gentleman of the game, a quality given official recognition with his knighthood in 1956.

Hutton posing for the photographers in 1951.

> " *I saw Len Hutton in his prime. Another time, another time.* "
>
> Harold Pinter

CRICKET
— SCORECARD —

Sir Len Hutton

Name: Sir Len Hutton

Born: 1916

Died: 1990

Test appearances: 79

Batting average: 56.67

Bowling average: 77.33

First-class batting average: 55.51

First-class bowling average: 29.51

> " *The greatest opening batsman I have ever seen.* "
>
> Denis Compton

ABOVE: Another English great of the 1950s and a key figure in the Test side's revival was Trevor Bailey. A brilliant all-rounder and yet another of those athletes who could combine a cricket career with talent on the football field (he won an FA Amateur Cup medal with Walthamstow Avenue), Bailey was nicknamed Barnacle for his tenacious, never-say-die qualities. In this photo from 1955, Bailey and his wife visited their son Kim at Southend hospital after he had been knocked down by a car.

RIGHT: The warm northern tones of Jim Laker provided the soundtrack for many an English summer, his relaxed and informed commentary for BBC television a wonderful counterpoint to the near hysteria of other entertainments. Yet the voice belied the ruthless ability of this devastating off-spinner to exploit a turning wicket. Laker famously took 19 wickets for a total of just 90 runs in his one-man humiliation of the Aussies in July 1956. He celebrated with a well-earned glass after taking all 10 Australian scalps in the second innings.

Cyril Washbrook was Len Hutton's stalwart partner at Test level. He wore his cap at a rakish angle and could play with a certain flair, as with this one-handed boundary in 1952.

ABOVE: Frank Tyson struck cold fear into the hearts of many a quivering batsman during the 1950s (with or without a spear). An erudite and educated man, "Typhoon Tyson" would quote Shakespeare before sallying once more unto the breach.

RIGHT: Australian great Richie Benaud thought Tyson was the fastest "quickie" he ever saw – and Benaud knew a thing or two about bowling. And batting, fielding and leadership on the pitch. A magnificent all-rounder, Benaud took Aussie cricket into a new age after the Bradman one had ended, skippering his side in brilliant style to win back the Ashes at the end of the decade. Like Laker, Benaud also became one of the most distinctive, shrewd and enlightening voices in cricket broadcasting.

—LEGENDS—

Fred Trueman

One of cricket's greatest ever bowlers and one of British sport's most compelling characters, Fred Trueman said it like he bowled it: hard, fast, often belligerently, but with considerable intelligence, faithful to his beliefs and keeping in the spirit of his surname. "Fiery Fred" was true to himself and personified his home county of Yorkshire – he was determined, outspoken, often uncompromising, yet possessed of a sharp wit and a straight-talking style that often pitted him against stuffy authority, making him a hero to his many, many fans. "Use every weapon within the rules and stretch the rules to breaking point, I say," advised Fred, and his blunt ways served him supremely well over a brilliant playing career and thereafter made him one of the most refreshingly honest of all commentators.

The first bowler to take 300 Test wickets, Trueman played for his country for 13 years, mostly glorious, though not always filled with success. He endured a mid-1950s spell out of the Test team but roared back in 1957 and became one of the first names the selectors turned to, even if some among their number blushed and bridled at his no-nonsense manner and what they saw as his occasionally wayward behaviour. With his trademark tousled dark hair trailing in the wind as he thundered in with all the force his 13-odd stone could muster, Trueman provided a highly individual sporting spectacle – and his passing robbed cricket of one of its most colourful and entertaining veterans.

Trueman had an array of talent at his disposal: he added variety and guile to his textbook bowling action as well as raw power.

"A cricketer walks into a pub . . ." Fiery Fred was a natural raconteur and funny man, and would have made for an excellent stand-up comedian.

> " *Fast bowlers are a breed apart, and Fred Trueman was apart from the breed.* "
>
> Denis Compton

BELOW: Trueman was tailor-made for presenting the traditional working man's pursuits such as darts. The much-missed *Indoor League* in which Fred celebrated a variety of pub games including skittles and arm wrestling made him a cult hero, together with his "I'll si thee" catchphrase.

CRICKET
— SCORECARD —

Fred Trueman

Name: Fred Trueman

Born: 1931

Died: 2006

Test appearances: 67

Batting average: 13.81

Bowling average: 21.57

First-class batting average: 15.56

First-class bowling average: 18.29

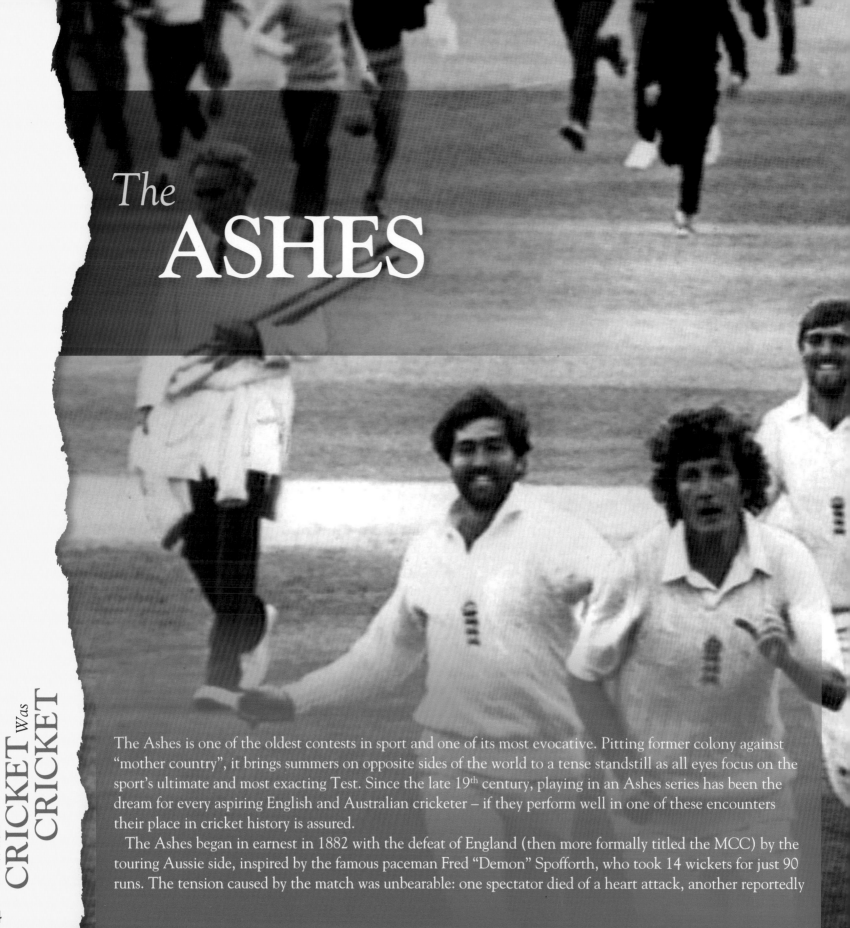

The ASHES

The Ashes is one of the oldest contests in sport and one of its most evocative. Pitting former colony against "mother country", it brings summers on opposite sides of the world to a tense standstill as all eyes focus on the sport's ultimate and most exacting Test. Since the late 19th century, playing in an Ashes series has been the dream for every aspiring English and Australian cricketer – if they perform well in one of these encounters their place in cricket history is assured.

The Ashes began in earnest in 1882 with the defeat of England (then more formally titled the MCC) by the touring Aussie side, inspired by the famous paceman Fred "Demon" Spofforth, who took 14 wickets for just 90 runs. The tension caused by the match was unbearable: one spectator died of a heart attack, another reportedly chewed through an umbrella. Such was the dismay at the humbling of the nation's sporting elite by a team still disregarded by some Englishmen as oikish upstarts from a fly-bitten outpost of the empire that mock obituaries were written and, later, a bail was burned, with the remains placed in a small urn to symbolize the death of English cricket.

The rivalry that has ensued has always been a keen one, illustrated by gleeful "pommie bashing" and "convict" teasing, but occasionally it has spilled over into out-and-out conflict. England and Australia may be two nations that share a common tongue and a love for cricket, but when the umpire calls "play" on the first day of an Ashes Test, the fun and games really begin…

Joy unconfined. The 21ˢᵗ July 1981 and Bob Willis leads Graham Gooch, Mike Gatting and Peter Willey in the victory charge off the pitch after beating Australia at Headingley – a famous game in a memorable Ashes series. Willis had just taken an incredible 8-43, to seal an astonishing England fightback after following on, inspired by Ian Botham, whose coruscating 149 not out in the second innings had rescued England from a seemingly impossible situation: at one stage they were given odds of 500-1 to win.

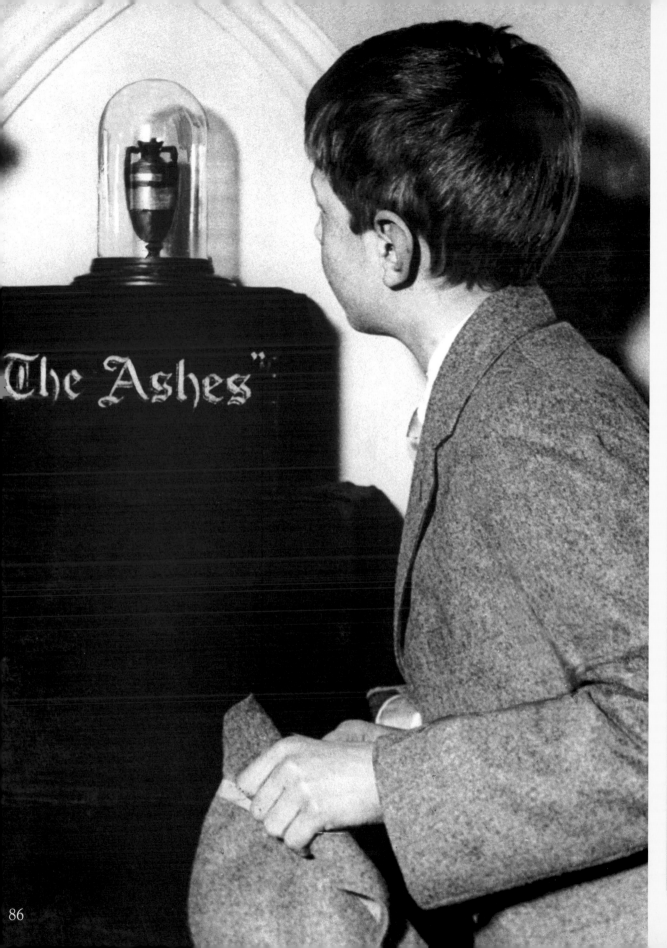

LEFT: A fragile little terracotta urn standing just a few inches high is what the fuss is supposedly all about.

Nearly 125 years after the first Ashes encounter, one of its legendary figures received a modern homage at the 2005 Test at Trent Bridge. W G didn't actually feature in very many Ashes matches (20 in total), but he made a dramatic impact in the pivotal game in 1882. He unsportingly stumped Sammy Jones, who was down the wicket tending a scrap of ground between deliveries. This so incensed the Aussies that it allegedly prompted Spofforth to wreak vengeful havoc among England's batting order.

The aim of English cricket is, in fact, mainly to beat Australia.

Jim Laker

Bodyline

The great Don Bradman slips at the wicket to avoid being hit by a ball from England's Bill Voce during England's tour of Australia in 1932-33.

It was this kind of delivery that made the series so infamous. Determined to negate the threat of Bradman and make the most of Aussie wickets that tended towards the predictable, England's captain Douglas Jardine (inset) had helped to devise a more aggressive variation on "leg-theory" strategy. Though he denied the specific intention, batsmen were targeted by swift, short deliveries, with a compact on-side field gathered at close quarters to pick up any loose defensive shots the man on strike might play to avoid being hit by the ball (this kind of field setting was banned in 1947).

It was a ruthlessly effective method. Australian batsmen suffered a battering: Bradman's average was cut down to 56.57 and England won the series 4-1. Jardine may have been vindicated by the result, but anger over his tactics led to a diplomatic storm and vilification at home and abroad. Australian fans, no respecters of assumed rank and privilege, despised the unrepentant Jardine for his superior airs and graces – and the hatred was mutual.

> "
> I've not travelled 6,000 miles
> to make friends. I'm here to win
> the Ashes.
>
> Douglas Jardine
> "

Australia's skipper Bill Woodfull took evasive action to avoid this bouncer from Bill Voce in the first Test at Sydney during the Bodyline series. Voce, his fellow Nottinghamshire bowler Harold Larwood and Bill Bowes were professionals who did as instructed by their captain and bowled according to the new strategy; Gubby Allen refused, but as an amateur he could express his opinion and countermand his captain's instructions.

RIGHT: The aggressive bowling wasn't all one way: Allen (later Sir Gubby Allen) received one where it hurts from Australia's Lisle Nagel.

By 1934 when Australia returned to England, the controversy had lessened, due in no small part to Jardine diplomatically not playing in the series on home soil. If there were more lasting victims of the Bodyline controversy, Voce and particularly Larwood (right) were the fall guys. The MCC wanted to make an example of the pair and asked the bowlers to apologize. Both refused, claiming that they had simply obeyed their captain's instructions. Larwood ghosted some newspaper articles defending his position, earning the lasting enmity of the powers that be. He never played for England again.

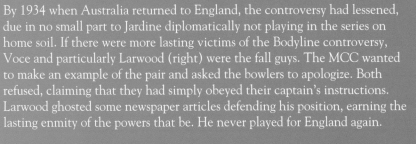

Life became sweeter for Larwood in retirement; he moved to Blackpool to run a confectionery shop and then in 1949 emigrated – to Australia, of all places.

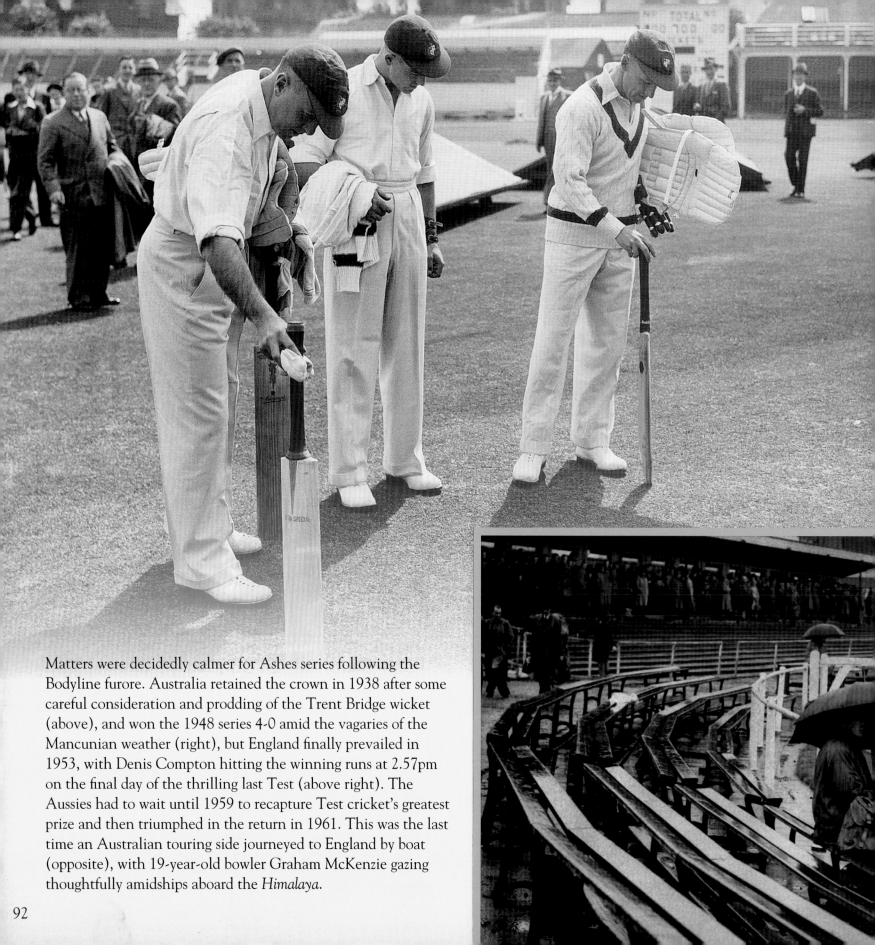

Matters were decidedly calmer for Ashes series following the
Bodyline furore. Australia retained the crown in 1938 after some
careful consideration and prodding of the Trent Bridge wicket
(above), and won the 1948 series 4-0 amid the vagaries of the
Mancunian weather (right), but England finally prevailed in
1953, with Denis Compton hitting the winning runs at 2.57pm
on the final day of the thrilling last Test (above right). The
Aussies had to wait until 1959 to recapture Test cricket's greatest
prize and then triumphed in the return in 1961. This was the last
time an Australian touring side journeyed to England by boat
(opposite), with 19-year-old bowler Graham McKenzie gazing
thoughtfully amidships aboard the *Himalaya*.

ABOVE: The 1975 series in England captured the front-page headlines after an extraordinary incident at Headingley. Intruders campaigning for the release of convicted armed robber George Davis broke into the ground on the night of 19th August and proceeded to dig up the pitch and pour oil over one end of the wicket. The match was ruined and England were thus robbed of the chance of a victory that might have provided the springboard for winning back the Ashes, much to the disgust of captain Tony Greig (right) seen here with his opposite number Ian Chappell (though rain that final day would have washed the match out in any case).

RIGHT: The centenary Test in 1977 saw the Don take centre stage at the MCG. With due reverence for the occasion, the Ashes were not actually at stake for this one-off match, won by the hosts by 45 runs.

> *The last positive thing England did for cricket was to invent it.*
>
> Ian Chappell

Beefy's Ashes

The Ashes has provided the appropriate stage for some of cricket's greats to shine, but few have dazzled as brightly as Ian Botham. The consummate all-rounder and one of the finest Englishmen to ever pick up a bat or deliver a ball, Botham was born to play in Test matches and ideally equipped to face the Aussies head on, matching their will-to-win with a determination almost uncharacteristic for men of his nationality. Matches against Australia were "Beefy's" forte and his performances in them provided the sport with some of its most extraordinary spectacles.

Having arrived on the county scene with Somerset as something of a prodigy, he made his Test debut against the Aussies in 1977 and immediately recorded a "five-for". His powerful batting, expert swing bowling and quick-witted brilliance in the field made him a shoo-in for the captaincy, which duly arrived in 1980. It was perhaps the only Test-format requirement he struggled with, and the disastrous start to the 1981 home series led to his swift resignation following a stony silence from the crowd after his pair at Lord's.

Relieved of the burden of formal leadership as the steady and highly capable Mike Brearley took his place, Botham instead led by example and played like a man possessed. In a trio of unforgettable matches he grabbed the starring role with bat and ball. His courage, fortitude and talent came to the fore, inspiring his team-mates and ending with a previously unthinkable 3-1 series win from 1-0 down with four to play. It was the "phoenix from the Ashes" series to end all series.

For anyone else, subsequent contests would have proved an anticlimax, but while Botham never quite hit the same heights, he still dominated cricket as the game's leading player for another decade. He became the first cricketer to reach 3,000 runs and take 300 wickets, and finished with a Test career total of 5,200 runs and 383 wickets. Quite simply, there will never be a player quite like Ian Botham.

"Hooowwwzaaaat!" Ian Botham was a fierce competitor and a born winner. His unbeaten 149 in the third Test of 1981, 5 wickets for 11 runs in the following rubber at Edgbaston, and magnificent 118 at a frenzied Old Trafford in the next was the stuff of cricketing fairytales.

> "If you're playing against the Australians, you don't walk.
>
> Ian Botham

–LEGENDS–

Sir Ian Botham

Like father, like son: for a while it looked as if Liam Botham might follow in his dad's not inconsiderable footsteps, but, like his football-playing dad, he was a chip off the old block and proficient in a number of sports, including rugby, in which he made his name.

> *A Test match without Ian Botham is like a horror film without Boris Karloff.*
>
> Fred Trueman

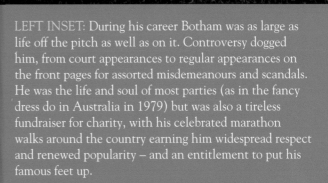

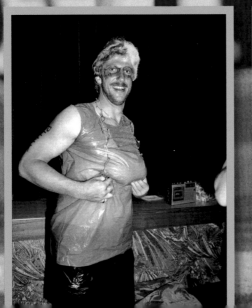

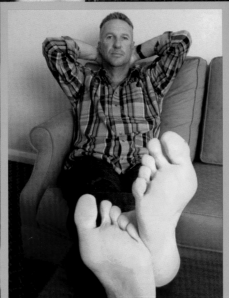

LEFT INSET: During his career Botham was as large as life off the pitch as well as on it. Controversy dogged him, from court appearances to regular appearances on the front pages for assorted misdemeanours and scandals. He was the life and soul of most parties (as in the fancy dress do in Australia in 1979) but was also a tireless fundraiser for charity, with his celebrated marathon walks around the country earning him widespread respect and renewed popularity – and an entitlement to put his famous feet up.

It wasn't all sweetness and light during the 1981 Ashes series. In the second Test at Lord's frustrated fans threw cushions onto the pitch in protest at bad light stopping play on the second day.

SUPPORT CRICKET
JOIN MIDDLESEX C.C.C NOW!

ABOVE: During one drinks interval Australia's famously combative wicket-keeper Rodney Marsh remonstrated with a fan after a ball had been picked up before it had crossed the boundary rope. "You stay on your side of the fence, we'll stay on ours!", Marsh fumed.

BELOW: All is fair in love and war – and sometimes the Ashes. While the rivalry has on occasion spilled over into anger and downright hostility, English and Australian players have by and large got along well enough. After the tumultuous 1981 series drew to a close in a drawn game at the Oval, the camaraderie between opposing players was there for all to see.

The
1960s

It was the decade that swung and when Western society threw off the shackles of conformity and tradition. At least in some circles. Yet while cricket retained much of its traditionalist core, it too began to yield to the forces of change, with increasing commercialism and development, and a reach that was spreading beyond its more familiar bastions of power. This was the decade in which the West Indies emerged as one of the strongest forces in world cricket, acting as the springboard for a reign that was to last for the best part of two decades.

The Windies began the 1960s by taking part in the remarkable first ever tied Test, recorded in **1960** in Brisbane against Australia. This thrilling contest seemed to lift Test matches out of what had been a relative slump in terms of excitement. In **1961** Australia retained the Ashes, the highlight of which was a blistering spell by Richie Benaud who took 5 for 12 with just 25 balls in the fourth Test. Yorkshire won the county championship that same year and again in **1962**; they were to win it a total of six times during the 1960s.

1963 saw the archaic distinction between amateur and professional cricketers finally abolished in English cricket. In another change that would have sent the Colonel Blimps of the old guard into spluttering bewilderment, one-day cricket made its debut with the first major tournament: the Gillette Cup. Sussex were the first winners, beating Worcestershire by 14 runs.

That same year, in further recognition of the elevation of the West Indies to the top tier of the game, *Wisden* marked its 100th edition by presenting the Wisden trophy, for Test matches between England and the West Indies. In **1965** Ceylon, Fiji and the USA became first associate members of the ICC, and in **1968** another broom swept through the corridors of English power, as the Test and County Cricket Board replaced the English Board of Control.

The decade drew to a close on a political note. After years of campaign pressure against apartheid, and following the Basil D'Oliveira affair, the **1968-69** MCC tour of South Africa was cancelled. The South Africans would not be officially welcomed back into the fold for a generation.

Ecstatic crowds invaded the Oval pitch in 1963 after the West Indies beat England to complete a 3-1 series win and lift the first Wisden trophy.

ABOVE: Sampling the televised delights of the FA Cup final in May 1961 were members of the victorious Australian touring side and Yorkshire CCC. Among the group are Peter Burge (Aus), Ken Taylor, Doug Padgett and Jimmy Binks (Yorks); middle row, Ron Gaunt (Aus), Phil Sharpe (Yorks) and Brian Booth (Aus); at rear is Yorkshire's Brian Stott.

LEFT: With Hawkeye and the referral system just a glint in various boffins' eyes, umpires were still the (usually) venerated arbiters of cricket's ancient laws. At a school for umpires in January 1966, the next batch – including, shock of all shocks, a woman – received their learned training.

ABOVE: The scientific types were at it again in the summer of 1966. Bernard Flack, from the University of Wales, took soil samples from the Warwickshire CCC wicket in order to help find out what made a good pitch.

LEFT: Technology waited for no man, however. Also in 1966 a group of white-coated men tested out their new electronic device to measure the speed of a fast bowler.

Women had been playing cricket since at least the 1740s, and with the sexual and gender revolution of the 1960s the presence of the fairer sex within the game began to be more keenly felt. Women still had some way to go, however – the ban on females becoming members of the MCC was still in force.

> ## Do women players wear protective boxes?
> – Interviewer
> "Oh yes. We call them manhole covers."
> – Heyhoe-Flint *

(* this quote has also been attributed to that driest and most urbane of cricketing wits, David Gower)

ABOVE: Struggling to gather some enthusiasm for their task were two Test match score recordists, sitting beside their equipment in 1968. Callers could phone the service to find out the progress of play.

LEFT: One of the great names in female cricket has been Rachel Heyhoe-Flint, seen here in 1968 leading out an International XI to take on a men's team in Whitmore, Staffordshire. Heyhoe-Flint played for England for over 20 years, was skipper for 12 of those, and was the first woman to be inducted into the ICC Hall of Fame. "Professional coaching," she once said, "is a man trying to get you to keep your legs together when other men have spent a lifetime trying to get them apart."

Woman to the rescue... In 1964, the dreadful batting form of Martin Walter Ltd's cricket team led to the employment of a female player to teach the team a few batting basics. Former Kent Ladies XI star Jean de Vere did her best to help them recover after they were bowled out for the handsome score of 0 in a game against local rivals Saltwood. Martin Walter Ltd fared better in the next match, hitting 30 runs for 3 wickets before rain stopped play.

The familiar tale of a washout at Southport in July 1967, when a flooded pitch put paid to the game between Lancashire and Kent.

Some things never changed: Yorkshire players used old-fashioned methods to dry out their pitch in August 1966.

Taking in the rays at Old Trafford in June 1969, one happy spectator dressed for the English summer in typical British style.

ESSEX COUNTY
CRICKET CLUB
—
DONATIONS
FOR SUNDAY
CRICKET

A spectator digs deep for some change to make his donation in order to watch the Essex v. Somerset match on 16th May 1966 – the first to be played on a Sunday. The "donation" was a means to get around Sunday trading laws, and 6,000 contributed for the match at Ilford's Valentine Park.

Praise Be!

Cricket has often been seen by its most devoted believers as God's own game, and men and women of the cloth have often combined their faith with a love of the sport.

Sister Gabriel was a coach of the school cricket team at St Josephs School, Bradford in June 1964.

Perhaps the most famous cricketing cleric was the Reverend David Sheppard. Pictured here in 1962 at the Mayflower Family Centre of which he was Warden, Shepherd deputized as captain for England twice, played in 22 Tests and was a much-loved batsman for Sussex. He later became a popular Bishop of Liverpool.

Conrad Hunte was a West Indian batsman of considerable repute, a fearless shot maker who took the fight to the bowler. He was similarly committed with his Christian faith, and read a lesson to a different sort of audience at Manchester's Albert Hall in June 1966.

> *Cricket is a game which the English, not being spiritual people, have invented in order to give themselves some conception of Eternity.*
>
> Lord Stormont Mancroft

A Game Apart

The issue over South Africa and its hated system of apartheid was one of the keenest of all cricketing controversies. Throughout the 1960s pressure began to build on sporting bodies to take a stance against the country's policy of racist segregation against the black majority.

Matters came to a head with the D'Oliveira affair that focused attention on the English cricketing establishment to break off cricketing connections. Eventually, after discussions with the British government and a debate in Parliament, the powers that be relented and official tours were cancelled under a ban that was to last over 20 years.

South Africa's ostracism was tough on its cricket team, just as it was forming a decent side featuring the likes of outstanding batsman Graeme Pollock, and controversial rebel tours were held throughout the period of exclusion. But it is widely regarded that the exclusion of South Africa from the world of cricket and other sports played a part in the final dismantling of apartheid.

Basil D'Oliveira, seen here with a group of children in 1967, was propelled into the apartheid furore in 1968. A South African and categorized as a "Cape coloured" under the regime's bizarre system of racial classification, D'Oliveira was effectively barred from any chance of competing for the nation of his birth and so emigrated to England in 1966. He was chosen to play for England, but was left out of the 1968-69 touring party to South Africa, amid accusations that the MCC had colluded with the apartheid government to exclude him on racial grounds. Eventually, under intense public scrutiny, the MCC relented and D'Oliveira was called up for the tour.

Vorster, prime minister of South Africa, accused the MCC of selecting D'Oliveira for political reasons, and the tour was cancelled. The issue brought matters to a head, with figures such as the Reverend David Sheppard and future England skipper Mike Brearley vociferous in their support for ending the tours.

Anti-apartheid demonstrations against South African teams had been held since the early Sixties, as with this protest outside Edgbaston in June 1960. With the "Stop the Tour" campaign in 1970 against the proposed visit by South Africa to England, the English cricket authorities finally conceded the issue and the series was cancelled. The affair also spelled the end for the MCC's long control over English cricket, then ceded to the Cricket Council and the Test and County Cricket Board (TCCB).

All-Round Brilliance

There are all-rounders – and then there is Garry Sobers. No other cricketer has matched the complete range of talent that Sobers had at his disposal. In isolation, his skills were remarkable – put together they made him a phenomenon.

He was one of the game's best-ever batsmen with a fluent, left-handed style that he could switch to devastating attack when and where he wanted; his versatile bowling was lethal, by turns a mastery of left-arm spin producing bewildering chinamen and googlies, a style that could be transformed in an instant into devilish medium-paced swing or rippling fast deliveries; in the field he was wonderfully athletic and one of the safest pair of hands a fellow bowler could wish for.

With such an extraordinary combination of skills, he was setting records and the cricket world alight within a couple of seasons of his emergence on the first-class scene. At 21, he hit an unbeaten 365 against Pakistan, a Test record that was to last for nearly 40 years. He smashed 226 against England in the 1959-60 series as part of a record stand of 399 with Frank Worrell. Most famously, he hit poor Malcolm Nash for six sixes in one incredible over for Nottinghamshire against Glamorgan in 1968, the first time the feat had been achieved at first-class level. He was also the first batsman to pass 8,000 runs in Test cricket.

Sobers' personality and sporting approach to the game helped turn him first into a hero for the West Indies and then for the world at large, privileged to have seen him in his prime.

RIGHT: Named among *Wisden's* five greatest players of the 20th century, Sobers could switch from elegant, technically perfect stroke play to all-out assault at the crease.

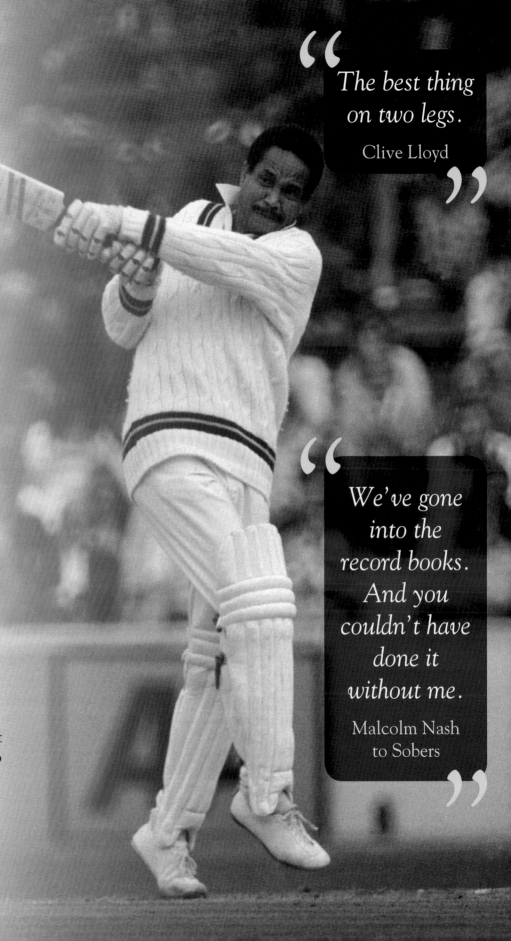

> " *The best thing on two legs.*
>
> Clive Lloyd "

> " *We've gone into the record books. And you couldn't have done it without me.*
>
> Malcolm Nash to Sobers "

–LEGENDS–

Sir Garfield Sobers

BELOW: A tragic episode in Sobers' life came in 1959, when he was involved in a car accident that ended in the death of team-mate and close friend Collie Smith, himself an outstanding all-rounder. Sobers was the driver of the vehicle and was fined for driving without due care and attention; Sobers said he had been blinded by oncoming headlights. He is pictured here with fellow cricketer Tom Dewdney.

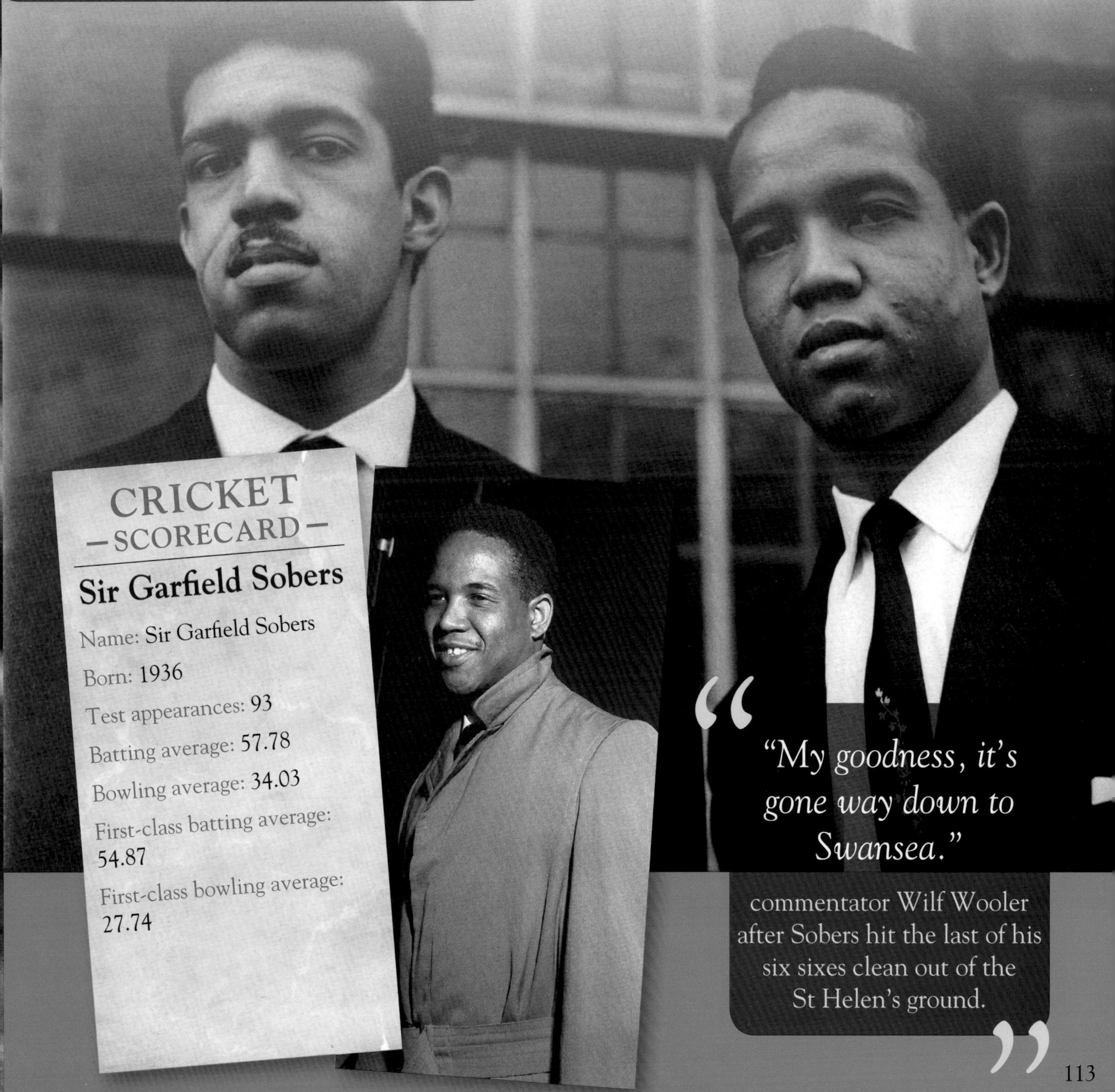

CRICKET
–SCORECARD–

Sir Garfield Sobers

Name: Sir Garfield Sobers

Born: 1936

Test appearances: 93

Batting average: 57.78

Bowling average: 34.03

First-class batting average: 54.87

First-class bowling average: 27.74

> "My goodness, it's gone way down to Swansea."
>
> commentator Wilf Wooler after Sobers hit the last of his six sixes clean out of the St Helen's ground.

113

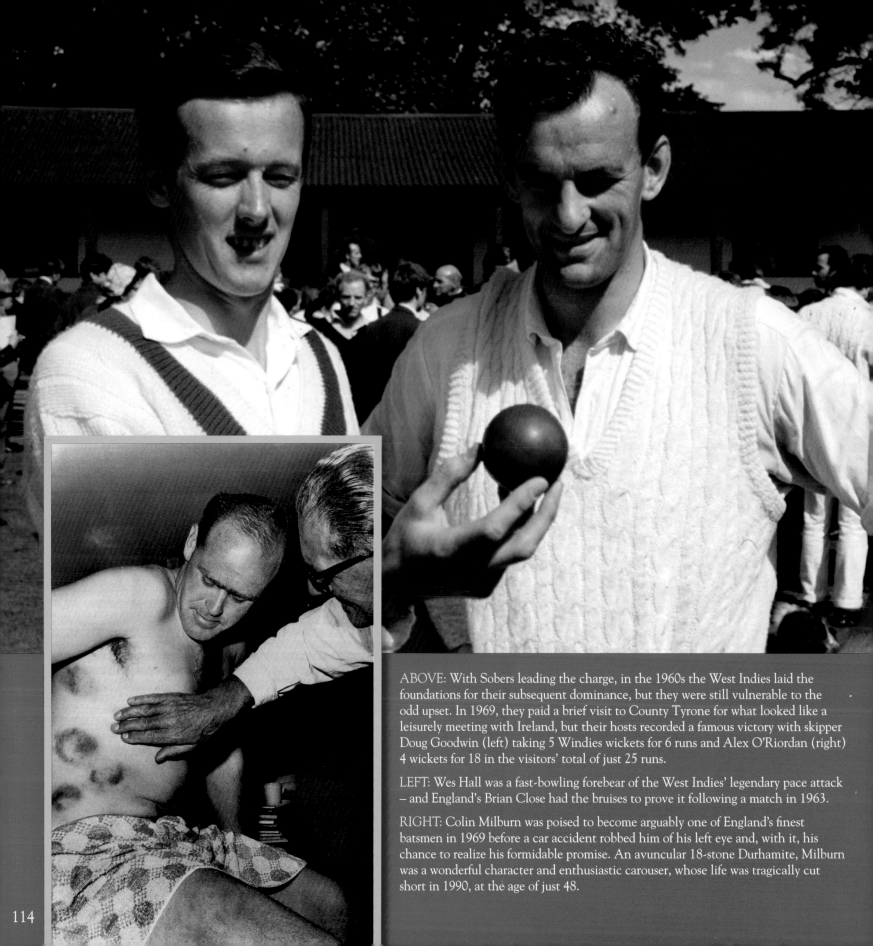

ABOVE: With Sobers leading the charge, in the 1960s the West Indies laid the foundations for their subsequent dominance, but they were still vulnerable to the odd upset. In 1969, they paid a brief visit to County Tyrone for what looked like a leisurely meeting with Ireland, but their hosts recorded a famous victory with skipper Doug Goodwin (left) taking 5 Windies wickets for 6 runs and Alex O'Riordan (right) 4 wickets for 18 in the visitors' total of just 25 runs.

LEFT: Wes Hall was a fast-bowling forebear of the West Indies' legendary pace attack – and England's Brian Close had the bruises to prove it following a match in 1963.

RIGHT: Colin Milburn was poised to become arguably one of England's finest batsmen in 1969 before a car accident robbed him of his left eye and, with it, his chance to realize his formidable promise. An avuncular 18-stone Durhamite, Milburn was a wonderful character and enthusiastic carouser, whose life was tragically cut short in 1990, at the age of just 48.

> "A great gust of North-East fresh air."
>
> John Arlott, on Colin Milburn

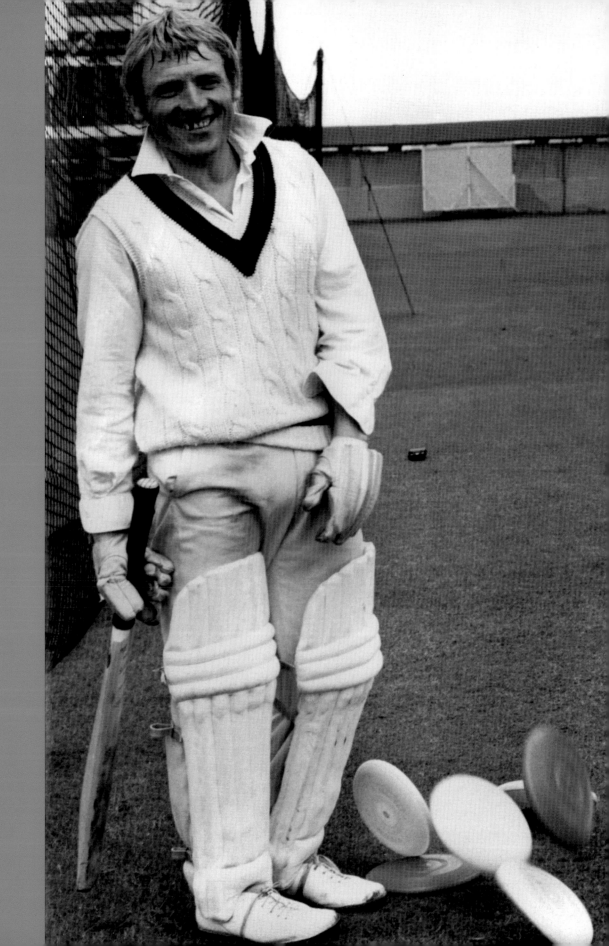

RIGHT: As the decade drew to a close, not even cricket was immune to the wackier crazes of the period. The Frisbee was presented to an ever-so-slightly wowed British public in June 1969 with a rather literal launch at Old Trafford. "It soars, curves, and dives like a typical UFO" ran the spiel. Old W G would have been spinning in his grave.

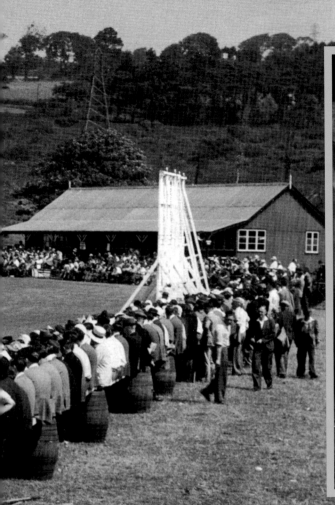

Glamorgan's tour through South Wales took in Cardiff Arms Park for its home matches for over 40 years. In 1966, the club left the site for pastures new at Sophia Gardens, with cricket on the Arms Park site making way for the new rugby development. To mark the occasion, a ceremonial burning of stumps by members of the Cardiff and Nomads teams took place on 17th September 1966.

Cricket was first played on common ground and public open spaces, with some sites dating back to at least the 17th century. The practice continued with the Regent's Ladies Games Club playing their matches in Regent's Park in 1909.

ENGLAND v. AUSTRALIA

ABOVE: Temporary sheds, together with grass roofs, were erected at the Sinhalese Sports ground in Colombo, Sri Lanka, for the visit of the MCC in October 1958.

LEFT: Sydney Cricket Ground, seen here in 1930, is one of the sport's most famous venues. The site first hosted first-class matches in 1878.

RIGHT: Worcester's Cathedral has provided the picturesque backdrop for county matches in the city. The New Road venue welcomed Don Bradman to the crease for the match against the touring Aussies in May 1930.

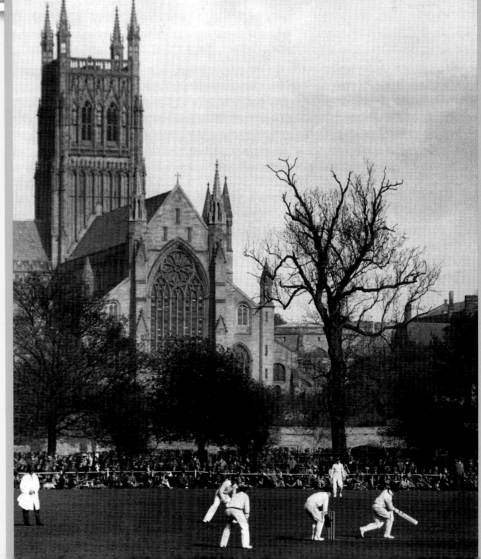

Headingley in 1935. The ground was not Yorkshire's HQ at the time – that honour went to Bramall Lane from 1863, which hosted county matches for 110 years, sharing the site with Sheffield United FC and their three-sided-ground on an adjoining pitch.

LEFT: By 1973, the forces of football had put to an end the practicality and financial viability of playing cricket at Bramall Lane. The final county match – a drawn Roses tie against Lancashire – took place on the 4th–7th August, and saw some fans dig up little mementoes of 118 years of cricket history in the city of steel.

LEFT: One fan taking it lying down was this gentleman for the opening day of the season at Cambridge University's famous Fenners ground, during the 1987 match against Essex.

RIGHT: Cricket was first played at Old Trafford in 1857. In July 1964, the car park outside provided the venue for an impromptu match before the fourth Ashes Test.

League cricket in the north of England has a long and illustrious history. It is arguable that the roots of the English game lie in the urban environment of northern towns and cities as much as in the gentler rural surroundings of the south. Manchester's Longsight Cricket Club first opened its gates in 1848, and in 1953 a match was played against an industrial landscape of factory chimneys. Sadly, the venue closed for cricket in 2004.

Castleton Moor were members of the Central Lancashire League between 1916 and 1987. Formed in 1858, the club had a ground in Rochdale that had a unique, homely but no-nonsense charm, as illustrated here in 1953.

Buxton's hills gave a 1939 match between Derbyshire and Lancashire a beautiful setting.

127

Alan Knott hard at it in the gym. Knott was a brilliant protégé of Evans, inheriting his position behind the wicket for Kent and England.

Gray-Nicolls have been synonymous with cricket bats for nearly 70 years (with the Nicolls' name enjoying an even longer lineage: the company started making bats in the 1870s and supplied W G Grace with his record-breaking bat in 1894). By 1975, the partnership's factory in Robertsbridge, Sussex, was a hive of craftsmanship, with Ted Jolly, 62, working on the revolutionary "Scoop" bat.

135

–LEGENDS–

Geoffrey Boycott

Geoffrey Boycott was another proud son of Yorkshire who appeared to embody the singular characteristics that county wants to see in its sporting heroes. Uncompromising, single-minded, and resolutely determined, Boycott had the necessary traits that turned a promising opening batsman into one of the sport's finest exponents of the art.

A prodigious run-getter, he scored 151 first-class centuries and for a while was the most prolific of all Test batsmen, retiring with 8,114 to his name. Key to his success was his timing, his masterful levels of concentration and his dogged refusal to give his wicket away cheaply. Boycott treated his time at the crease as precious and woe betide anyone who wanted to take it away from him. This led to accusations that he would slow the run rate down to a crawl, and Ian Botham even claimed to have deliberately run "Boycs" out in a match against New Zealand.

Passed over as England captain, Boycott spent three years out of the Test side between 1974 and 1977, but was then recalled to become a central figure in the England team until 1982. Since then he has been one of the most outspoken yet perceptive of commentators.

RIGHT: With a stump and a glass of champagne, Boycott celebrated his 100th century in the decisive Test of the 1977 Ashes, scored on his beloved home ground of Headingley.

> "Of all the great players I have seen, if I had to pick a batsman to bat for my life, I would go for Geoffrey."
>
> Dickie Bird

CRICKET
— SCORECARD —

Geoffrey Boycott

Name: Geoffrey Boycott

Born: 1940

Test appearances: 108

Batting average: 47.72

Bowling average: 54.57

First-class batting average: 56.83

First-class bowling average: 32.42

ABOVE: Cricket might have lost one of its greatest batsmen to football had it not been for his eyesight. Boycott had dreamed of playing professional football but in an age before the advent of suitable contact lenses he had to wear glasses, which meant he opted instead for the summer game.

Boycott reaching 100 again against the Aussies in 1980.

Devastating Den

> " *Ashes to Ashes, dust to dust, if Thomson don't get ya, Lillee must.*
>
> *Sydney Telegraph, 1975 Ashes* "

ABOVE: In 1972, Ted Dexter was one of many to be on the receiving end of a Lillee delivery.

Who's afraid of big, bad Dennis Lillee? For a period straddling the 1970s and 1980s, this fiery Western Australian was one of the most potent forces in cricket, a viciously quick paceman who could wreak havoc through even the most resilient of batting orders. In tandem with Jeff Thomson (with Rod Marsh providing able catching support behind the stumps), Lillee formed an attack that developed into one of the greatest ever bowling partnerships, a pair of long-haired rebels ripping through batting orders around the world.

Blessed with an impeccable technique, aggression, tenacity and that almost genetic will to win instilled into his countrymen, Lillee looked the part of a demon fast bowler with his dark features and bristling moustache. He tore through England in the 1974-75 Ashes series and was similarly devastating against the more resolute West Indies the following season. He finished with a record 355 Test wickets to his name, but this record might have been even higher had he not suffered a serious back injury that was to flare up throughout his career, nor had he been one of the star names who accepted Kerry Packer's invitation to join the WSC.

Lillee was a player who made headlines even without the ball. His aluminium bat caused an outcry, his physical confrontation with Javed Miandad earned him censure, and he famously had a bet of 500-1 against his own side during the 1981 Headingley Test. But it was behaviour that in truth only added to his iconoclastic allure.

–LEGENDS–

Dennis Lillee

Australian crowds loved their menacing paceman.

BAR

DEADLY DENNIS

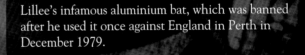
Lillee's infamous aluminium bat, which was banned after he used it once against England in Perth in December 1979.

CRICKET
– SCORECARD –

Dennis Lillee

Name: Dennis Lillee

Born: 1949

Test appearances: 70

Batting average: 13.71

Bowling average: 23.92

First-class batting average: 13.90

First-class bowling average: 23.46

Lillee's fast-bowling partner Jeff Thomson got a quick hair cut from skipper Greg Chappell in preparation for the fourth Test in August 1977.

BELOW: In 1978 Dennis Amiss wore a "specially designed skull dome" – aka a helmet – for protection. Helmets were introduced to guard against the fearsome deliveries such as the likes of Lillee could produce.

In an age of lethal fast bowling, England's David Steele adopted a phlegmatic approach and played with his glasses on in the 1975 Ashes series against Australia. Steele's steadfast performances – his 365 in three Tests contributed to save England from a series defeat greater than the 1-0 margin – helped him become BBC Sports Personality of the Year the same year.

> *It's the easiest sport in the world to take over. Nobody bothered to pay the players what they were worth.*
>
> Kerry Packer

ABOVE: Kerry Packer (right) was the pugnacious media mogul who plunged cricket into a period of great turmoil during the 1970s. In 1976 his Channel 9 TV company bid to broadcast Test matches, offering the Australian Board a better deal than it had on the table from its long-standing partner, the national broadcaster. When the Board rejected Packer's proposal, he launched his own rival "super-Tests" series, signing up a number of star names including most of the Australian and West Indies' sides, plus high-profile cricketers from other Test-playing nations.

Former England skipper Tony Greig (left) was one of the best recruiters for "Packer's Circus", a star-studded and genuine rival to the established order with its day–night games, glitzy promotions and dramatic hard sell. After the TCCB tried and failed to ban players from taking part, and following two seasons of razzle-dazzle competition, Packer won a 10-year deal to finally broadcast official Test matches. Modern commercial might had won through, and the players were the real winners, seeing their wages rise dramatically.

RIGHT: When "normal" Test cricket resumed, Australian and English players joined forces for some fancy dress fun for Christmas 1979.

141

The faces of England's future: in December 1976, four young cricketers were presented at Lord's and tipped for great things. The quartet was selected under a scheme sponsored by Whitbread's, to gain experience playing in Australia. Bill Athey (second right) went on to play in 23 Tests; fellow Yorkshireman Graham Stevenson (far right) played twice for his country, while Ian Botham (second left) didn't fare too badly. Neither did the clean-shaven chap on the left, Mike Gatting.

BELOW: No slip ups here: in the Roses match of August 1973, Lancashire assembled a field of three slips and three gullies.

Seventies Stories

Keeping it very much in the family were the cricketing Telfers from Stamfordham in Northumbria, a clan that could rustle up a whole team between them.

ABOVE: Irene Lott struck a blow – or rather cut a victory – for long-suffering cricket widows when she took a saw to her husband Stuart's cricket bat in September 1973. Lott was a 28-year-old policeman who played minor counties cricket in Devon.

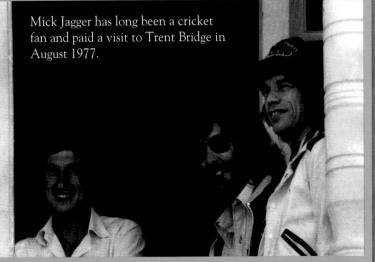

Mick Jagger has long been a cricket fan and paid a visit to Trent Bridge in August 1977.

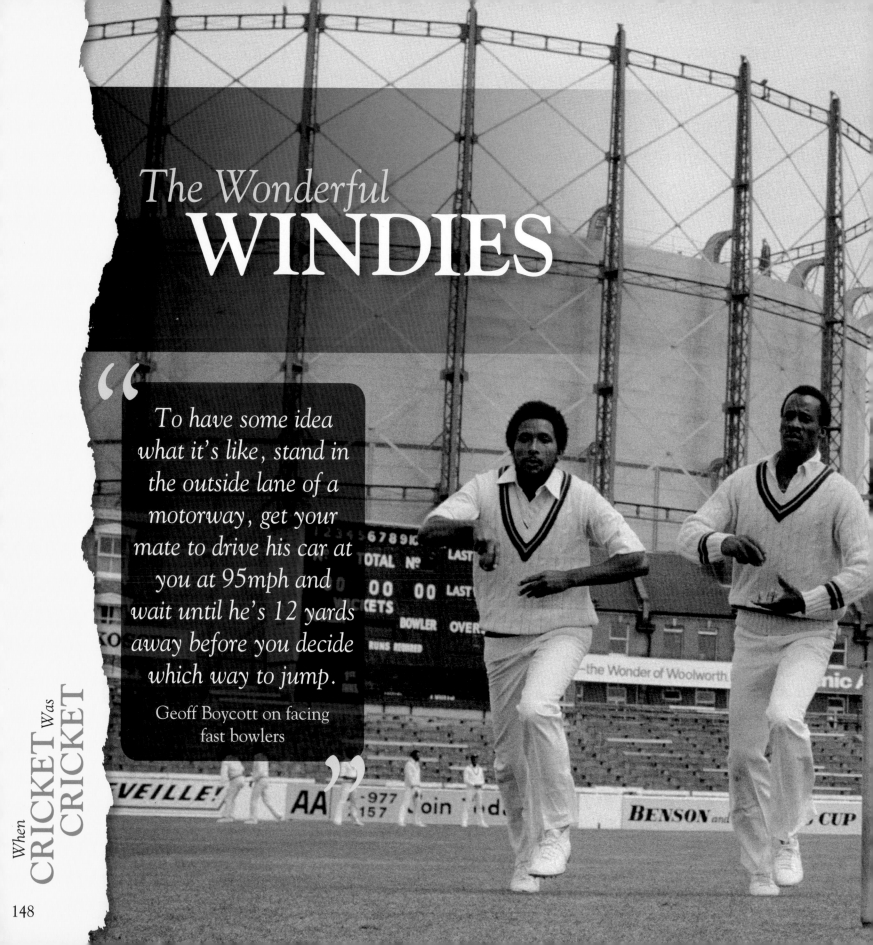

The Wonderful
WINDIES

> *To have some idea what it's like, stand in the outside lane of a motorway, get your mate to drive his car at you at 95mph and wait until he's 12 yards away before you decide which way to jump.*
>
> Geoff Boycott on facing fast bowlers

England might have given cricket to the world, but in the 1970s a collection of some of its smaller former colonies handed out a lesson to the mother country and the rest of the world in how to play the game. Despite a combined population of around just 4 million, the West Indies enjoyed a glorious period of dominance from the mid-1970s to the 1990s, giving to the sport some of its greatest individual performers and most brilliantly effective team units.

With bat and ball, and in the field, a succession of West Indian players put inter-island rivalry to one side and elevated a group of tiny countries onto the world stage.

Every batsman's nightmare: the fearsome four-man attack of (left to right) Andy Roberts, Vanburn Holder, Wayne Daniel and Michael Holding going through their paces at the Oval in May 1976, prior to winning the series 3-0 and so beginning the West Indies' long reign as the kings of cricket.

Sir (and later Baron) Learie Constantine presents the BBC Sports Personality of the Year award for 1963 to athlete Dorothy Hyman. Constantine was one of the first superstars to emerge from West Indian cricket, an outstanding all-rounder who would go on to build a distinguished career in politics. He was also a star performer with the great Northern League side, Nelson.

The West Indies arrive at London Airport in 1966 to do battle once more with England. English sport was on a high after the football team had won the World Cup that summer, but the Windies dampened celebrations with an impressive 3-1 series win.

Deadly Whispers

Andy Roberts and Michael Holding take an energetic seaside stroll at Hove just before renewing hostilities against England in the summer of 1976. The pair terrorized English batsmen during the tour. Roberts had ice running through his veins and his unrelenting precision allied to a devastating bouncer saw him take 28 wickets for an average of 19.71 runs. Holding proved even more effective with 28 victims for an average of just 12.71 runs, but he was the more long-lasting of the duo, continuing to cut a remorseless swathe through opposing batting orders until 1987.

The Oval, 12th–17th August 1976 and Holding bangs another one in (left) during one of the most devastating spells of fast bowling ever produced. Holding took a total of 14 wickets for just 149 runs – little over 10 runs apiece – bowling beautifully straight and fast on a pitch supposedly rendered lifeless by the long hot summer of that year.

Holding was nicknamed Whispering Death for his long and almost silent run-up, the smoothness of his approach only serving to make him even more terrifying to the batsmen on the receiving end of his killer deliveries. England skipper Tony Greig had infamously said before the series that he intended to make the West Indies "grovel", but it was Greig who was to bow down (below left), cleaned bowled twice by Holding.

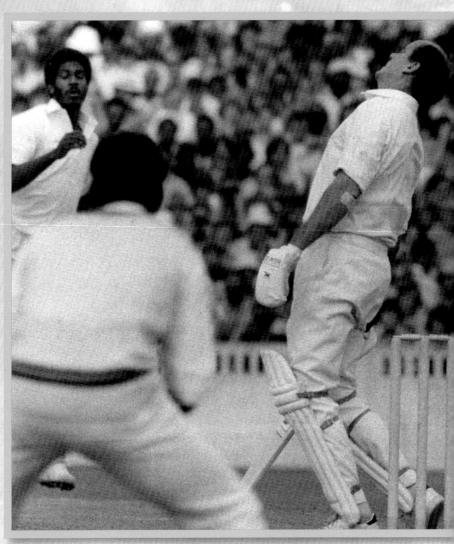

Holding was at his brutal best against Brian Close, no stranger to being on the receiving end of a battering (see pages 114–15). In the third Test at Old Trafford, Holding produced one of the most ferocious overs with a short-pitched assault that in some quarters drew comparisons with Bodyline.

Captain Fantastic

At first glance Clive Lloyd may not have seemed the most natural of athletes, and with his glasses and gentle demeanour he appeared to be anything but fearsome, but looks and impressions can be deceptive. Lloyd was a terrific player, an astute tactician and one of the most successful of all Test captains.

It was Lloyd's brilliant leadership that played a major part in turning a team of many individual talents into a cohesive and thrillingly exciting whole. Lloyd was an accomplished left-hander and his whip-crack reflexes in the field earned him the nickname of Supercat. Under his tenure, the West Indies purred. Taking over the captaincy in 1975, Lloyd announced his intent with a succession of centuries including 242 not out against India, before inspiring his side to victory in the first ever World Cup final in 1975.

Thereafter, Lloyd and his side didn't look back. Yet more series wins and another World Cup followed; in 1984-85 Lloyd presided over the first of two 5-0 thrashings meted out to England, each dubbed the "blackwash" series. In the same period Lloyd won 11 Tests on the spin and was unbeaten in 26. He engineered the side's superiority over what was a considerable Australian outfit and took on and defeated all-comers, to the extent that the Windies became near invincible.

CRICKET
— SCORECARD —

Clive Lloyd

Name: Clive Lloyd

Born: 1944

Test appearances: 110

Batting average: 46.67

Bowling average: 62.20

First-class batting average: 49.26

First-class bowling average: 36.00

–LEGENDS–

Clive Lloyd

Whispering Death takes a well-earned rest after the completion of the 3-0 series win over England in 1976.

BELOW: Another Windies triumph, another dressing room celebration. England players including Greig and Alan Knott sportingly offered their congratulations after the visitors won by 158 runs at the Oval in 1973.

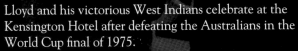

Lloyd and his victorious West Indians celebrate at the Kensington Hotel after defeating the Australians in the World Cup final of 1975.

All Rise for the West Indies

The exciting spectacle of the West Indies on the field was almost matched by the entertainment provided by the team's supporters off it. Ebullient, vocal and loud in their acclaim for their heroes, Windies fans introduced a blast of raucous fresh air into the more reserved and often staid atmospheres of English Test grounds. The noise and enthusiasm didn't always go down too well with the stuffier members of the cricket establishment, but most England fans appeared to revel in it.

157

For black communities across the country, whether first-generation immigrants from the Caribbean and elsewhere, or subsequent generations born and brought up in Britain, the West Indies were a source of immense pride.

"

I do it for the people.

West Indies fast bowler Curtly Ambrose, 1994

"

West Indian glories were to fade as the modern team struggled, but those images from the side's heyday will live long in the memory of those who were there to witness them, whichever team they supported – like these England fans (below) scattered among a jubilant crowd in front of the Oval pavilion in 1973.

> "What do they know of cricket who only cricket know?"
>
> C L R James

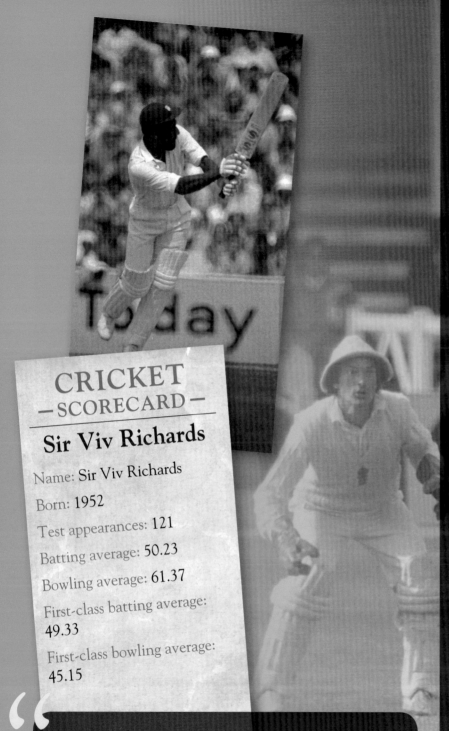

–LEGENDS–

Sir Viv Richards

If West Indian bowlers gave their utmost in demonstrating how seamers could intimidate and defeat batsmen, Vivian Richards showed how to return the favour. Over a 22-year first-class career, this Antiguan hero reigned as one of the world's finest, and as captain cemented the West Indies' position as the best side in the sport.

The second West Indian to be featured in *Wisden*'s greatest players of the 20th century, Richards hit 24 Test centuries, smashed an average of 118.42 during the thumping series win over England in 1976, hit 138 not out from just 157 balls in the 1979 World Cup final, and took on and tamed the fastest of bowlers from Lillee to Hadlee. The statistics, impressive as they are, don't tell the whole story. Coming in at number three with a trademark swagger, he was a joy to watch at the crease, whatever the format. Exceptional timing, athletic power, savage force when it was required and astonishing reflexes together meant he could tame even the fiercest and most cunning of bowlers. Brave to the point of reckless – he never wore a helmet – Richards met the age-old challenge of batsmen versus bowler and invariably came out as the victor.

Such performances were not just one-man displays of mercurial talent. In so utterly destroying the spirit of opposing bowlers, he forced them onto the defensive and made life easier for his team-mates. Job done. Picking up the captain's baton full-time from Lloyd in 1985 was the natural progression, and Richards instilled perhaps an even greater degree of pride in what the West Indian players were representing. Of all the famous Windies batsmen of the 1970s–1990s, from Greenidge and Haynes to Adams and Lara, Richards was the best of the lot. Indeed, his good friend Ian Botham said Richards was the "best player that ever lived", and there would be few to dispute the claim.

CRICKET
– SCORECARD –

Sir Viv Richards

Name: Sir Viv Richards

Born: 1952

Test appearances: 121

Batting average: 50.23

Bowling average: 61.37

First-class batting average: 49.33

First-class bowling average: 45.15

"

They [bowlers] get six deliveries so they can afford mistakes. We [batsmen] only have one life.

Viv Richards

"

Great players, superb teams, epic contests, further rebel tours and not a little controversy: the 1980s might not have satisfied the arch purist, but it was a decade packed with talking points and memories to savour. While the West Indies continued their era of near invincibility, the other Test nations competed on a relatively equal footing. Possession of the Ashes switched between England and Australia, while India and Pakistan's equally close-contested rivalry meant bragging rights between the two ebbed and flowed, with other countries joining the international cricket set.

As if to signify the changing times, **1980** saw an arcane relic of previous years finally consigned to history when the eight-ball over was abolished in Australia. **A year later**, underarm bowling was specifically outlawed; this followed the infamous ODI between Australia and New Zealand, when Trevor Chappell was ordered by his brother Greg to bowl the final ball of the match underarm and so deny New Zealand the chance to tie the match.

New faces appeared on the scene: Sri Lanka made their Test debut in **1982**, while Zimbabwe played their first ODIs in **1983**. Zimbabwe caused a sensation in the World Cup that year by beating Australia, but it was India who ended the West Indies' reign as champions in the final. Sri Lanka's first Test victory followed in **1985**.

A second ever Test draw came in **1986** when India and Australia tied at Madras. Another milestone came that year when Viv Richards became the first player to take five wickets in a one-day innings and score a century. Australia served notice of their emergence as the coming force with victory in the **1987** World Cup, but perhaps the most famous international clash of that year came with Mike Gatting's incendiary row with Pakistani umpire Shakoor Rana.

Less of a headline-grabber was the commencement of four-day games in the English county championship in **1988**. Someone who would go on to make many more headlines was Sachin Tendulkar, who in **1989** scored his first Test 50, aged just 16.

In the heat of the night: floodlit cricket came to England with a *Daily Mirror*-sponsored challenge match between Essex and the West Indies at Chelsea FC's Stamford Bridge stadium on 15th August 1980. Graham Gooch's century set the evening alight in front of a crowd 11,000 strong.

When CRICKET *was* CRICKET

David Gower in disconsolate pose in 1989.
Sadly, this was an all-too familiar sight
for England fans. Gower embodied the
contradictions that lay at the heart of much of
the nation's cricket. A stylish classicist with
the bat, Gower was at one stage the world's
leading Test-runs maker, a beautifully composed
left-hander who with his elegance and style
appeared to be a throwback to the Golden Age.
Yet he could also be vulnerable at the crease
and his career with the England team, including
a spell as captain, coincided with a period of
inconsistency and decline for the national side
despite the presence of gifted individuals.

Though he won a series in India and led
England to Ashes victory in 1985, Gower was
twice on the receiving end of 5-0 drubbings from
the all-conquering West Indies. The close to
his England career was in keeping with its ups
and downs: flying a Tiger Moth aeroplane and
buzzing the ground in Queensland where his
team-mates were playing was a stunt that led to
his eventual removal from the side.

> *You can make plans
> but if the opposition plays
> well, then all your plans
> become worthless.*
>
> David Gower

167

England Faces

LEFT: Former England skipper Mike Brearley in jovial mood for a Middlesex photocall in 1981, wrapping up against the February chill. Brearley was not the greatest of players but was a superb captain for county and country. A scholarly man with a First in Classics from Cambridge, he was an expert man-manager and has enjoyed a subsequent career as a leading psychoanalyst.

> *He has a degree in people.*
>
> Aussie fast bowler Rodney Hogg on Brearley

RIGHT: Bob Willis' extraordinary bowling performances in the 1981 Ashes series invited comparisons with the skill of a snake charmer.

ABOVE: In his benefit year, Willis turned up for a fund-raising function dressed as a koala bear. At the same do, Dennis Lillie signed autographs on ladies shoes.

RIGHT: The West Indies' reign at the head of international cricket was almost unrelenting. An assembly line of great players maintained the side's brilliant consistency. Joining skipper Clive Lloyd (far right) for a Bridgetown warm-up in 1981 were Joel Garner and Colin Croft.

ABOVE: Roland Butcher made history by becoming England's first black player, debuting in the 1980-81 series in the West Indies.

LEFT: Media centre, West Indies style.

–LEGENDS–

Malcolm Marshall

For a Test side that has produced so many great fast bowlers, it is testament to Malcolm Marshall's supreme talent that he should be regarded as the West Indies' greatest ever paceman. Indeed for some observers he was the finest fast bowler of any side. That he was ferociously quick and could intimidate with a vicious bouncer was almost a given, but Marshall had so much more in his armoury, possessing a dazzling complement of skills that has made him so revered. A lack of height suggested he should have struggled to produce shorter deliveries of real venom, but if anything his size aided his ability to conjure up something different.

With 376 Test wickets to his name, Marshall was one of the West Indies' most prolific bowlers, and the most adaptable. Even on benign pitches he could devastate batting orders. English batsmen were among his most embattled victims, like the seven who succumbed for just 22 runs in a famous spell at Old Trafford in 1988. If the essence of cricket is a contest of wills between batsman and bowler, Marshall was one of its most intelligent of practitioners. No mean run-maker himself, he could discern the slightest weakness to incisive and ruthless effect.

The tragedy is that Marshall is spoken of in the past tense. He died of cancer in 1999 aged just 41, and a measure of his popularity was the sadness that marked his passing, not just in the West Indies and at Hampshire where he played county cricket, but around the world. The founding of the Malcolm Marshall trophy, awarded to the leading wicket-taker in a West Indies versus England series, was fitting memorial to a special cricketer and a much-missed man.

Celebrating taking yet another England scalp, this time that of Alan Lamb.

In his day he was unplayable.

Ian Botham

CRICKET
— SCORECARD —

Malcolm Marshall

Name: Malcolm Marshall

Born: 1958

Died: 1999

Test appearances: 81

Batting average: 18.85

Bowling average: 20.94

First-class batting average: 24.83

First-class bowling average: 19.10

ABOVE: Robin Smith and Viv Richards took part in the Malcolm Marshall memorial match at the Artillery Club London in 2000, the pair pictured here with Malcolm's son Mali.

RIGHT: England's Mike Gatting was one of many Marshall victims, and returned home sporting a battered nose after being on the receiving end of a 90mph Marshall special in February 1986.

Cricketing Gear and Garb

Cricket's global family continued to grow. Players from Fiji wearing traditional national dress, the "sulu", instead of the usual whites, arrived at Heathrow in June 1982 for the ICC Trophy tournament.

LEFT: 71-year-old Tom Lawford ended his 60-year amateur career in 1980 with a ceremonial burning of his whites.

BELOW: The market for cricket memorabilia and collectables got a boost with the bicentenary of the MCC in 1987. A linen commemorative handkerchief printed in purple from 1785 was expected to fetch £10,000.

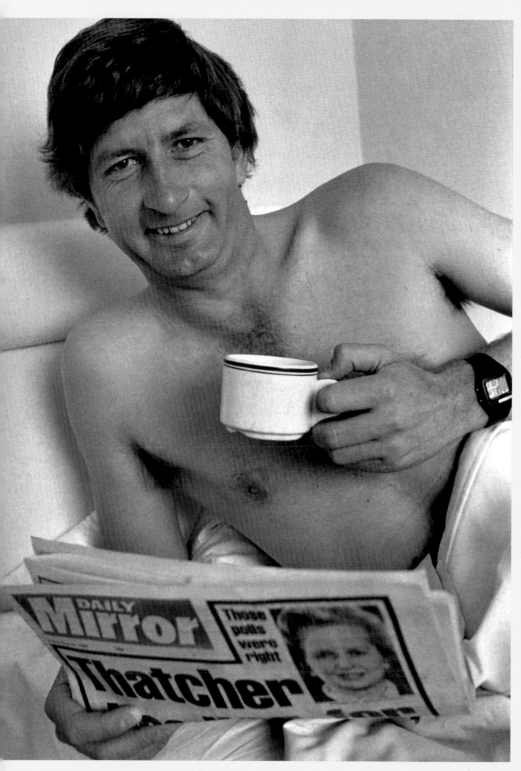

Eighties Faces

Who's that with a cuppa and a copy of the *Daily Mirror* in his Nottingham hotel in June 1983? It's Duncan Fletcher, then captain of Zimbabwe and future England coach.

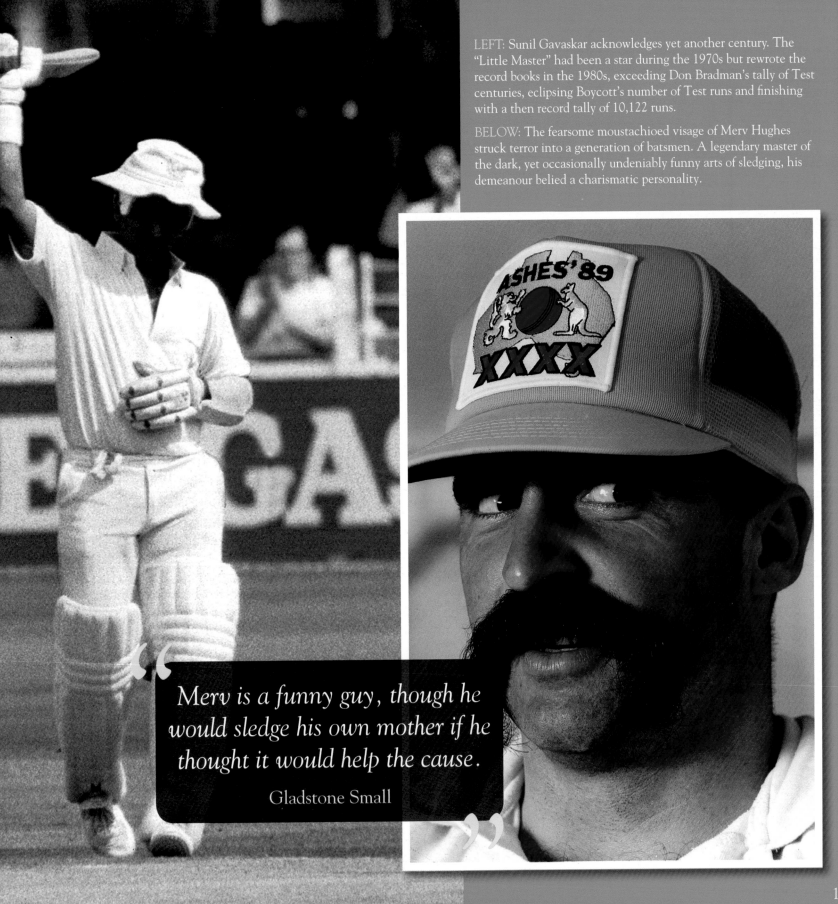

LEFT: Sunil Gavaskar acknowledges yet another century. The "Little Master" had been a star during the 1970s but rewrote the record books in the 1980s, exceeding Don Bradman's tally of Test centuries, eclipsing Boycott's number of Test runs and finishing with a then record tally of 10,122 runs.

BELOW: The fearsome moustachioed visage of Merv Hughes struck terror into a generation of batsmen. A legendary master of the dark, yet occasionally undeniably funny arts of sledging, his demeanour belied a charismatic personality.

"Merv is a funny guy, though he would sledge his own mother if he thought it would help the cause."

Gladstone Small

177

–LEGENDS–

Imran Khan

A dashing hero with an all-round acumen for cricket and for life outside the game, Imran Khan came to the fore as one of the world's leading players in the 1980s and played a crucial part in establishing Pakistan as a major power. As captain, his performances with bat and ball enabled his nation to compete with – and beat – the best.

Imran came from a family steeped in cricket and his success in the game seemed almost predetermined. Yet he took a while to settle and establish himself, only cementing a place at the third time of asking in 1976-77, though Pakistani sporting intrigue would still occasionally disrupt his progress. But with his displays, Imran eventually became an indispensable fixture in the team and he captained the side to successive series victories over India and Australia, drawn series with the otherwise omnipotent Windies, and further triumphs including the World Cup in 1992. Such success was made all the more remarkable by the judgement that the Pakistan side Imran skippered was not a particularly great one – he simply knew how to get the best out of team-mates and led by example.

After cricket, Imran's fame if anything burgeoned. He entered the risky world of domestic politics, married Jemima Goldsmith and strode the international scene of both statesmanship and celebrity status.

CRICKET
– SCORECARD –

Imran Khan

Name: Imran Khan

Born: 1952

Test appearances: 88

Batting average: 37.69

Bowling average: 22.81

First-class batting average: 36.79

First-class bowling average: 22.32

LEFT: Imran in free-flowing action for Pakistan against Surrey at the Oval in 1982.

BELOW: Whether on the field of play or in the somewhat more dangerous field of politics, Imran Khan has always looked at home, as with this TV interview with Sir David Frost.

It's Not Quite
CRICKET

While cricket's illustrious heritage is presented as an exemplary reflection of the more venerable traditions of sporting life, there have been plenty of occasions when the game has lent itself to the comical, the untypical and the downright farcical.

Displaying more of a *pas de deux* than an opening partnership, two members of the Festival Ballet Company sported pads and bats for a rehearsal at Eltham.

BELOW: 1958, and the Lord's Taverners take on the American Yaleman in a culture clash of cricket and gridiron.

Animal Antics

Dog stopped play?
Animal trespasses are as
old as the game itself,
and this Jack Russell did
what a dog's got to do
when caught short in
November 1975.

Two primates who were king of the swingers in 1953.

The annual Brambles sandbank match has been a fixture of the seaside summer since the 1950s. The game is played between the Royal Southern Yacht Club and the Island Sailing Club on a sandbank that appears at yearly low tides between Southampton and the Isle of Wight. Matches, like the one pictured here in September 1966, are limited to as many overs as can be packed into the half hour the "pitch" is playable.

ABOVE: A fresh-faced Jonathan Agnew at Leicestershire, before he became the master of ceremonies for the modern TMS.

Tales from the Commentary Box

One of cricket's most enduring customs is its commentary. Whether in print, on radio or TV, and now online, the journalism and literature surrounding the game has established a reputation as venerable as the sport it covers. Foremost among the institutions dedicated to covering and discussing the game has been the BBC's Test Match Special.

Featuring the varied tones (ranging from dulcet to the occasionally grumpy) from a succession of ex-pros and esteemed journalists, TMS has been a part of the broadcasting landscape since 1957, providing reliable expert comment and diverting gentle humour. In essence it has lived up to Lord Reith's doctrine that the BBC should "educate, inform and entertain". Extended praise for homemade cakes and the occasional outburst of infectious giggles (most famously from Johnston and Agnew) might not be exactly what Reith had in mind in entertainment terms, but TMS has become a genuine national treasure.

LEFT: One of TMS's finest field placings: left to right: Peter Baxter, David "Bumble" Lloyd, Don "The Alderman" Mosey, the legendary Brian "Johnners" Johnston and Fred Trueman wax lyrical from the commentary box in August 1990.

BELOW: John Arlott, seen here casting an independent expert eye over proceedings from the press box at Lord's in June 1980, has been described as the greatest cricket commentator. Arlott was a multi-talented broadcaster, author, poet, campaigner and wine connoisseur, but he was never more at home than when writing or talking about cricket. Note the almost total absence of televisions, computers and assorted gadgetry in this scene: just one man and his notes and some of the finest words ever uttered about the game, in that wonderfully distinctive Hampshire burr.

> *Asif Masood approaches the wicket like Groucho Marx chasing after a pretty waitress.*
>
> John Arlott

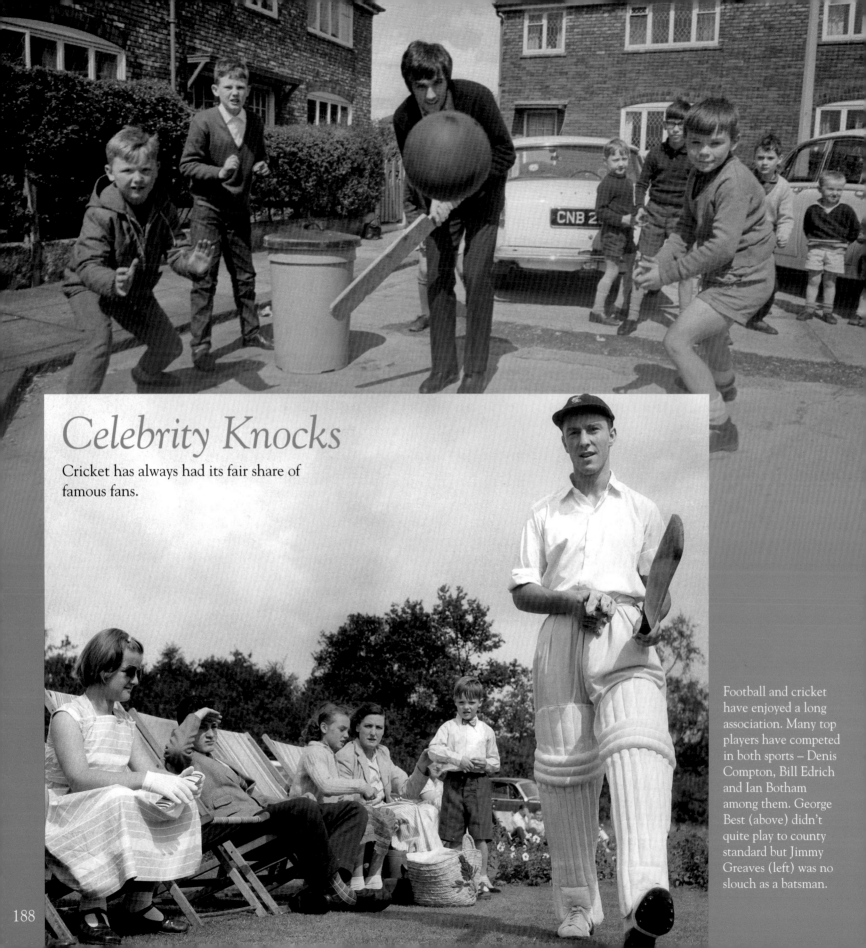

Celebrity Knocks

Cricket has always had its fair share of famous fans.

Football and cricket have enjoyed a long association. Many top players have competed in both sports – Denis Compton, Bill Edrich and Ian Botham among them. George Best (above) didn't quite play to county standard but Jimmy Greaves (left) was no slouch as a batsman.

And its "howzat!" from him: Ronnie Corbett keeps wicket behind Peter Willey during England's tour of Australia in 1979-80.

ABOVE: Cast as the new Doctor Who in 1981 was Peter Davison. The fifth incarnation of the Timelord was a cricket fan whose knowledge and love of the game would occasionally help him out of tight corners.

Actors like Peter O'Toole and Oliver Reed (below) have been prominent cricket supporters and occasional players.

English-born Bob Hope (centre) might have remembered a glimmer of cricket from his childhood past and perhaps Joan Collins too, but it all looked slightly alien to Bing Crosby in 1961.

ABOVE: Who's a chirpy chappie, then? Much-loved umpire Harold "Dickie" Bird, met Oscar the parrot, one of the feathered friends Bird was judging as part of a panel to find Britain's champion chatterbox bird in December 1989.

RIGHT: Being England captain, his country's record Test run-scorer and with 20 Test centuries to his name didn't save Graham Gooch from the dubious honour of featuring as a *Spitting Image* puppet in November 1991.

Fashion Faux-Pas

Cricket and fashion are not the most obvious of partners but every now and then the two worlds collide. In 1959 designers turned to the game for inspiration for some ladies' wear.

RIGHT: Changing and more permissive times caused a stir in 1998 when model Debbie-Lee, 28-year-old girlfriend of Aussie and Essex cricketer Stuart Law, posed at the home of cricket during a Lord's-hosted lingerie fashion event. While many traditionalists would have viewed such goings on as sacrilegious, Lee struck a blow for female liberation: during the show she was able to nip off and tread the hallowed surroundings of the Lord's pavilion at a time when women were still banned from becoming members of the MCC. It wasn't until March 1999 that women were finally admitted into the club as full members.

MEMBERS ONLY

Not quite so sartorially elegant as Debbie-Lee was former Glasgow Govan MP, the Badar Islam – a huge cricket fan in several senses.

ABOVE: A modern trend has been to don fancy dress for a day at the cricket. In July 1988 one pair of intrepid fans had a less than happy experience. A pantomime cow at the fourth Test at Headingley was rugby tackled by stewards at close of play and Brancha Resic, drawing the short straw and occupying the rear end, had to be taken to hospital with serious neck injuries.

RIGHT: Cricket's sometime clown prince was Derek Randall, whose occasionally brilliant feats with the bat (he scored 174 in the Centenary Ashes Test) could be matched by a repertoire of outlandish tricks.

OPPOSITE: Cricket fans can be an obsessive bunch, but who would want a few cuttings from the Lord's wicket in 1968? Plenty, judging by the prolific bagging up going on here, as souvenir packages were sealed up to be sent around the world.

There's nothing quite like an English summer and a sweltering day at Lord's for the second Test against Australia. On 2nd August 1975 the sun is out and all eyes – well, a few – are fixed on the on-field action.

The
1990s

Someone with a landmark date of his own in the 1990s was David Gower, who wed his partner Thorunn Nash in September 1992, with sporting colleagues such as Mark Nicholas, Robin Smith, Gary Lineker, Ian Botham, Alan Lamb and Bob Willis in attendance.

Night matches, garishly coloured kits, wall-to-wall satellite TV coverage, "stump cams", "snickometers", and mutterings of plans afoot to play matches limited to just 20 overs per side... Not every feature of modern cricket stems from the 1990s, but the decade ushered in a host of developments and innovations that, for some supporters at least, rendered the game a shadow of its former self. But in order to compete in the highly commercialized reality of modern sport, cricket needed to move with the times, and the 1990s was a period of significant and perhaps irreversible change.

The modern era began with one of the strangest overs in cricket history. In February **1990** Wellington's Bert Vance took the ball on the final day of his side's New Zealand Shell trophy match against Canterbury; in order to try to force a result that could benefit Wellington's quest for trophy success, Vance despatched a succession of full-toss no-balls; 22 deliveries later, Canterbury had scored 77 runs – from just five legitimate balls – before the bewildered umpire called a halt. A more welcome record was set that year when Sachin Tendulkar became the youngest player to score a Test century in England, 119 not out at the age of 17 years and 107 days; in the same series Graham Gooch scored a record aggregate of 456, including a memorable 333 in one innings.

Zimbabwe joined the ranks of Test playing nations in **1992**, while another newcomer made a more dramatic individual impact in **1993**, when Shane Warne delivered his famous "ball of the century" to dismiss Mike Gatting. In the same year the West Indies beat Australia in a Test by just one run and another amazing feat followed in **1994** when Brian Lara set a first-class world record of 501 not out.

Controversy followed in **1995** when umpire Darrell Hair no-balled Sri Lankan spinner Muttiah Muralitharan seven times for throwing in the second Test against Australia; Muralitharan survived the doubts over his action and went on to become the world's leading wicket-taker with 800 victims. Sri Lanka were caught up in further scandal when their **1996** World Cup semi-final against India in Calcutta was abandoned due to crowd trouble, but the Sri Lankan's went on to beat Australia in the final. Further Sri Lankan success followed in **1997** when the side produced the highest single innings Test score of 952-6 declared against India.

Pat Symcox might not quite have matched the Sri Lankans but his **1998** century for South Africa against Pakistan was no mean feat for a player batting at number 10. Also in **1998**, the BBC lost uninterrupted television rights to Test cricket to Sky and Channel 4, leaving the Beeb, after 60 years of broadcasting, with no live Test cricket. In **1999**, Bangladesh arrived on the international scene with victory over Pakistan in the World Cup.

English cricket suffered an indifferent period during the 1990s as the side struggled to compete with the leading nations, in particular Australia. Yet there were some successes, such as a welcome win in the first Test against the West Indies in March 1990. Celebrating at Sabina Park were (left to right) Devon Malcolm, Angus Fraser, Graham Gooch, Alan Lamb and Gladstone Small.

Sabina Park earned a sad place in cricket notoriety in 1998 when it hosted the first Test ever to be abandoned due to the dangerous condition of the pitch, an event which seemed to sum up the decline in West Indian cricket.

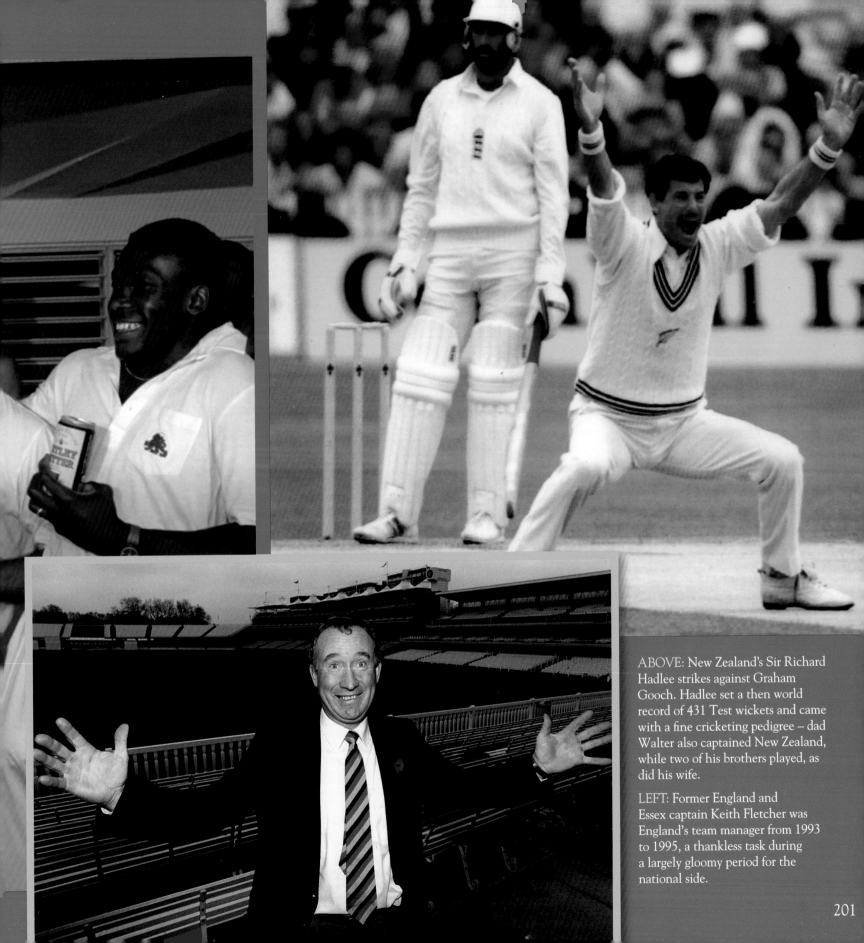

ABOVE: New Zealand's Sir Richard Hadlee strikes against Graham Gooch. Hadlee set a then world record of 431 Test wickets and came with a fine cricketing pedigree – dad Walter also captained New Zealand, while two of his brothers played, as did his wife.

LEFT: Former England and Essex captain Keith Fletcher was England's team manager from 1993 to 1995, a thankless task during a largely gloomy period for the national side.

A Little Master Among Men

The hands of the master.

CRICKET
— SCORECARD* —

Sachin Tendulkar

Name: Sachin Tendulkar

Born: 1973

Test appearances: 177

Batting average: 56.94

Bowling average: 53.06

First-class batting average: 59.86

First-class bowling average: 61.14

(* at time of writing, January 2011)

Yet another Tendulkar century, yet another boundary, this time during the third Test against England at Trent Bridge in July 1996.

—LEGENDS—

Sachin Tendulkar

The term "natural" is an oft and perhaps overemployed word to describe a performer of exceptional talents, but the term is entirely appropriate when discussing the merits of the great Sachin Tendulkar. A prodigious batsman from the unfeasibly young age of 12, he scored his first Test century at just 17 and has been carrying on in pretty much the same vein for India ever since.

Such were Tendulkar's exploits as a child that it was seen as a disappointment when he missed out on the 1988-89 tour to the West Indies at the age of 15. He did not have to wait long, however, to make a dramatic impact, and in 1989 took on Pakistan's brilliant triple pace attack of Waqar Younis, Imran Khan and Wasim Akram, and came through with distinction. His bravery is just one facet of his many extraordinary talents. He is a fluent stylist and a master of precision, an orthodox and diligent stroke-maker unafraid to let rip and take a game by the scruff of the neck, whatever the format, whatever the conditions. The result is the greatest batsman of modern times and a multiple record-holder: over 14,600 Test runs to his name, 51 Test centuries, the most centuries in ODIs, the first man to score a double century in an ODI.

At the time of writing Tendulkar is still playing at something like the peak of his powers; still racking up the mammoth scores and setting new benchmarks. For such a classically gifted batsman, he is a very modern sporting superstar – a demi-god in his native India and, for a naturally shy man, a global icon whose fame transcends his sport.

Brian Lara

Brian Lara was not just a phenomenal batsman but also a scorer of phenomenal runs. In isolation his joyous stroke play and thrilling power made him one of the greats; with his record-breaking displays of mammoth innings, he achieved cricketing immortality. That he should produce such epic performances in the midst of a period of decline for the West Indies makes his individual achievements all the more heroic.

Having already announced his greatness with a brilliant 277 against the outstanding Australian attack in 1993, Lara smashed two of the most sacred batting records within weeks of each other in 1994 – first with the marathon 375 against England that beat Gary Sobers' longstanding individual Test record, then with the unbeaten 501 for Warwickshire over Durham, a stunning display that left all sport agog at Lara's talent and its unrelenting application. When the Test record was taken by Australia's Matthew Hayden 10 years later, and with the West Indies facing a humiliating rout in the 2003-04 home series with England, Lara regained his crown with an unbeaten, incomparable 400.

At a troubled time for West Indian cricket, when disputes ruined team cohesion and morale, and the all-conquering sides of the past were becoming an increasingly distant memory, Lara singlehandedly restored pride and in the process made the game in general just that little bit more special.

RIGHT: Lara completing yet another century against England.

CRICKET
—SCORECARD—
Brian Lara

Name: Brian Lara

Born: 1969

Test appearances: 131

Batting average: 52.88

Bowling average: N/A

First-class batting average: 51.88

First-class bowling average: 104.0

"*I still don't think this 500 makes me a great cricketer. I've still much to learn.*"

Brian Lara

–LEGENDS–

Shane Warne

Shane Warne began his career as the blond-haired poster boy of cricket, the charismatic, chipper and occasionally chippy lad who seemed to have been plucked straight out of a file in cricket's central casting marked "Aussie sportsmen with attitude". He ended his career as one of the finest ever players, and deservedly placed in *Wisden's* pantheon of the five best cricketers of the 20th century. Not only had Warne been arguably the game's greatest bowler, he had rescued and restored the lost and dying art of leg spin.

Warne's rise was meteoric, as he won his first baggy green cap after just seven first-class matches. After a less than spectacular start, he arrived in England in 1993 with a burgeoning reputation but little to show for it. His first over removed any doubts as to his potential as he delivered what has been described as the "ball of the century" to utterly bewilder, confuse and dramatically remove Mike Gatting.

In tandem with wicket-keepers Ian Healy and then Adam Gilchrist, Warne was one of the most prolific, persistent and ingenious wicket-takers in the game, with 708 Test scalps succumbing to his leg breaks, drifters, flippers and assorted other deliveries that sometimes defied the laws of physics, let alone description. "Bowling, Warney!", uttered by colleagues as Warne bamboozled another poor victim, became part of the game's vernacular. He was just as deadly in the one-day game. And he could bat a bit – in fact he scored more Test runs (3,154 of them) without reaching a century than any other player.

No stranger to a juicy headline, connected either to cricket, women or some sort of caper or scandal, Warne was a pop-star player who attracted the attentions of big sponsors and was a key personality in enabling the commercial modernization of the game. He was no role model for the puritans, yet he enthralled even the starchiest of traditionalists. Though he remains one of the sport's most compelling characters, his talent was supreme and once he retired, Australia – and cricket – were a little less watchable for it.

> *How anyone can spin a ball the width of Gatting boggles the mind.*
>
> writer Martin Johnson

Warne celebrates *that* ball which dismissed a befuddled Mike Gatting (right) in 1993. The delivery had pitched outside leg stump and ripped back to knock down Gatting's off stump.

CRICKET
— SCORECARD —

Shane Warne

Name: Shane Warne

Born: 1969

Test appearances: 145

Batting average: 17.32

Bowling average: 25.41

First-class batting average: 19.43

First-class bowling average: 26.11

" *In the space of a short time, he's turned the game upside down, changed it in concept.* "

Richie Benaud

Warne in effervescent mood after his pivotal role in defeating the old enemy at Old Trafford in 1997, having taken nine English wickets in the match.

By the end of the 1990s, cricket was still very much recognizable as the game played two centuries before, yet a player of that time might have been staggered to see the sport's global reach in the modern age. He might also have been less impressed with some of the changes that had taken place. Yet in the guise of Andrew Flintoff, he would surely have recognized a very English cricketing hero in the making, for all ages.

End of play...

Acknowledgements

A special thanks to Alex Waters for his superb assistance with picture research, to Richard Havers for his support and expert assistance, and to Dave Scripps and all at Mirrorpix.

Thank you also to Paul Moreton, Kevin Gardner and all at Haynes; Lee Pinkus, Troy Hagan and Martin Cloake.

Select bibliography

The author is indebted to many and varied sources for facts, figures and confirmations. The limitations of space constrain the number cited, but the following have proved invaluable:

The Ultimate Encyclopedia of Cricket – Peter Arnold and Peter Wynne-Thomas (Carlton, 2003)
ESPN Legends of Cricket – Geoff Armstrong (Sue Hines/Allen & Unwin, 2002)
Anyone But England – Mike Marquese (Verso, 1994)
Barry Norman's Book of Cricket (Quercus, 2009)
Wisden on the Ashes – ed. Steven Lynch (John Wisden and Co., 2009)
Wisden Cricketers' Almanack (various editions)
Daily Mirror
Dictionary of 20th Century World Biography – edited by Asa Briggs (Longman, 1985)
Cricinfo.com
bbc.co.uk
Wikipedia.com